Kalpana Swaminathan lives in Mumbai. Since *Cryptic Death* (1997), Lalli has appeared in seven novels, the most recent being *Murder in Seven Acts* (2018). Kalpana's other novels are *Ambrosia for Afters*, *Bougainvillea House* and *Venus Crossing*, which won the Crossword Fiction Award in 2009.

Kalpana writes with Ishrat Syed as Kalpish Ratna. Their most recent work of non-fiction is *A Crown of Thorns—The Coronavirus & Us* (September 2020)

ALSO BY KALPANA SWAMINATHAN

Lalli Mysteries

Cryptic Death and Other Stories (1997)
The Page 3 Murders (2006)
The Gardener's Song (2007)
The Monochrome Madonna (2010)
I Never Knew It Was You (2012)
The Secret Gardener (2013)
Greenlight (2017)
Murder in Seven Acts (2018)

Fiction

Ambrosia for Afters (2003)
Bougainvillea House (2005)
Venus Crossing (2009)

Children's Fiction

The True Adventures of Prince Teentang (1992)
Dattatray's Dinosaur (1994)
Ordinary Mr Pai (1999)
The Weekday Sisters (2002)
Gavial Avial (2002)
Jaldi's Friends (2003)

Raagam Taanam Pallavi

Kalpana Swaminathan

SPEAKING TIGER

SPEAKING TIGER BOOKS LLP
4381/4, Ansari Road, Daryaganj
New Delhi 110002

Published by Speaking Tiger Books in paperback 2020

ISBN: 9789389958782
eISBN: 9789389958799

10 9 8 7 6 5 4 3 2 1

Typeset in Sabon LT Std by SÜRYA, New Delhi
Printed At: MP Printers (A unit of DB Corp. Ltd.) Noida 201305

This is a work of fiction. Names, characters, places and incidents either are the product of the author's imagination or are used fictitiously, and any resemblance to actual persons, living or dead, events or locales is entirely coincidental.

For

Savithri

In devotion.

[29 August 1930–23 February 2014]

This book could not have been written without Ishrat, who gifted me Ambarnath, and introduced me to the mystic world of Murugan.

Contents

Author's Note

The Murugan Story

Murugan of Tamilakam is older and more colourful than his Vedic version. In Tamil culture he represents language and poetry. The word 'Murugan' means beauty, and the god represents Beauty as Truth.

Murugan has six heads—each represents a siddha or spiritual attainment. Murugan myths are set in the Tamil countryside, and the six major shrines celebrate different myths. The central myth is the killing of the demon Surapadman, an incredibly evil monster who had wangled the boon of immortality from Siva.

Murugan's weapon is his shining spear, the vel, meant to pierce Illusion, and reveal the Truth.

Surapadman, who stands for Ego, is pierced by Murugan's vel, but since he's immortal, Siva converts him into two birds, the strutting rooster and the flaunting peacock, and grants Surapadman his final request that he may never be parted from the Truth. So the rooster flies on Murugan's standard as the peacock flies him around the world.

The devotees of Murugan play out this myth in the ceremony of Azhagu. The devotee, burdened with woes (symbolized in the yoke or kavadi) makes a pilgrimage to the shrine. Here he or she undergoes a ritual piercing with the vel. The Mayil Azhagan is a devotee pierced with the vel and a framework of hooks in the form of a fanned out peacock's tail.

Murugan is the subject of traditional Tamil poetry, folk songs and music, transcending the usual barriers of caste.

Raagam

Lalli was preparing to die.

Nothing warned me. Not her brief illness a month ago, not Savio's insomniac vigils, not Dr Q's unusual generosity with books.

July seemed more quiet than it had ever been. Rain muffled the raucous noises of the street. Its music restored a gentler landscape. The house, too, altered its pulse, and retreated into tranquillity. That suited me. After the alarm of Lalli's illness, I needed a blank page.

Absorbed in a new novel, I noticed nothing till it turned around and bit me. Words went wide, sentences spun askew, the plot skittered, unravelled and swung loose, and I turned as usual, to Lalli for solace.

It had been a particularly frustrating morning. I had burst in with my woes, when my voice died away as I caught sight of her, and the truth blazed with sudden clarity. The rain-lit room turned harsh and hyper-real as I took in my aunt's appearance. Her book had slid to the floor. Her eyes were far away. Every line of her slender frame was intent on something I couldn't see. I steadied myself, giddy with understanding.

The others had known it weeks ago.

Lalli was preparing to die.

There was no other term for it. She was not *dying*. Dying implies a passive helplessness. My aunt was energetically withdrawing from life.

She was not ill, although she ate hardly anything and slept not at all. She perched bright-eyed on the beige sofa, distant but courteous, acknowledging our attentions, and unobtrusively rejecting every one of them. She was not apathetic. She heard us out with interest, but volunteered nothing.

She seemed to have retreated to a place of no return.

I imagined how we might seem to her as she accelerated into this powerful new gravitational field, our diminished faces regressing faster than expected, so soon to be lost in her own blur of speed.

It was a terrifying thought. I suggested coffee. She answered, as I knew she would, 'Later.'

Dr Q's books, treasures, I should say, were at her elbow. She read greedily, at random, and then abandoned each book with a petulant push as if it had got in her way.

Savio sat up late, talking to her. When I woke up at five, he would be snoring on the sofa, legs sticking out a mile. Lalli was rooted in the balcony, staring at the rain. She would take her coffee tumbler from me, with the smile that ignited my day—but after a sip it remained untouched till I took it away.

I went crazy in the kitchen trying to conjure up something to her taste until she stopped me with, 'Please don't, Sita, it only makes it harder for me.'

Savio sternly ordered me to leave her alone. He did, and so did Dr Q—at least, they did their bit and bowed out reassured, by *what* I found very difficult to tell.

Dr Hilla Driver, Lalli's erstwhile friend, dropped in, only to prescribe useless vitamins. It hadn't been easy to persuade Hilla to come. 'No, morning's impossible, I have my yoga, and then it's a whirlwind,' she'd said when I called. 'Ill? Nonsense. Lalli's never ill. Oh well, I'll squeeze in a few minutes between appointments.'

Hilla didn't stay long. 'There's nothing wrong with Lalli,' she murmured as I saw her out. 'She's just throwing a tantrum. Old people do that off and on.'

'She's not old, and this isn't a tantrum,' I answered hotly. 'She hasn't slept for a week to my certain knowledge. She barely swallows a morsel or two.'

'Look, Sita, she isn't physically ill. She isn't mentally ill, either. This is entirely volitional. Only she can tell us why.'

'And she won't.'

Hilla shrugged impatiently. These days Hilla

spent more time on herself than on her patients. A vacuous hunk ogled me from the back seat of her luxurious new BMW as I left her at the gate.

'Hilla has a trainer,' I remarked.

'What's she training for?' Lalli asked with a flash of her old wickedness. But it didn't last.

It couldn't. Despite her iron will, she was worn out. She stopped talking. She began to drift, first into absent spells, and then into a restless drowsiness. I roused her much against my will to coax a sip of milk or fruit juice.

She didn't fight this off. It was necessary to power the exhausting rituals of personal care. It took her an hour to emerge from her room, bathed and dressed for the day.

I couldn't bear to see her usual brisk stride transformed into a hesitant shuffle. There were times when she sat up alert and expectant, as if listening for a distant note of music. It always eluded her. The lost look would return, her eyes glitter hard and angry. What could we do but retreat, defeated by her carapace?

Monday started the same way. Lalli hadn't been to bed. She was in the balcony, staring at the rain. She came in, picked up her coffee, inhaled the aroma and abandoned the tumbler. She sat on the beige sofa with a little of her old poise, as if about to begin a conversation. I waited, but after a while, she leaned forward to touch my cheek and waved me away.

Savio and Dr Q came in around lunch time. Lalli had fallen into either abstraction or sleep.

This far, Lalli had made all her own medical decisions, refusing tests and therapies. Dr Q was my only hope. The trust between them was absolute.

'What's making her do this, Dr Q?' I demanded.

He looked away sadly. It was his way of saying that was no question to ask her.

He sat by her now, his hand resting lightly on her hair. This unexpected intimacy filled me with dread. Savio and I made a pretence at eating in the kitchen, till he broke down, pushing his plate away. He didn't cry so much as dissolve. It was awful seeing his huge frame actually dwindle in a helpless crouch of grief.

'She won't say a word,' he wept bitterly. 'Why won't she tell me what's eating her? How can I ask her? What if—'

Lalli had barricaded herself against us all. I sensed that in all their years together, she had never done this to Savio. She had been parent, mentor and friend since he was fourteen. This abrupt exclusion baffled him. I had no comfort to offer. There was no amulet, no charm or apotropaic to ward off the evil eye. Only this limbo.

'Dr Q's doing blood tests,' Savio said at last. 'She hasn't let us in so far, but now—'

She could no longer resist.

She could no longer resist the intrusion of the caress, or of the needle. I was shocked to discover I resented that.

She endured them.

She endured *us*.

I couldn't bear that. I could never bear being endured.

When Savio and Dr Q had left, I stayed in the kitchen staring at my notebook. No thoughts came, no words scattered on the page.

The doorbell rang. Neighbours. Utkrusha, B Wing, was concerned. By now, Building *knew*.

It was Ponni Mami from upstairs. Her husband Ramachandran and his boon companion Patherphaker hesitated on the landing.

'We heard about Lalli,' Ramachandran said. 'Savio says it's nothing serious, but his face tells a different story.'

'What can we do?' Patherphaker joined in, adding cautiously, 'without intruding, of course. What can we do? Can missus help?' Manda Tai, unlike her twitchy husband, was stolid gold.

'No, no, we're fine,' I assured him. Lalli needed her space—how could I explain that to these kind souls? 'She's taking a nap right now.'

Ponni lilted down the stairwell, 'When she wakes up why not ask if she'd like some music?'

I doubted very much if she would, but promising to ask, I thanked them and fled.

Ponni and her husband Ramachandran were friends I treasured for their talents, but there our acquaintance stopped.

Ramachandran talked books. He read continuously, omnivorously, and reactively. He never lent his books—except to me. Apart from his reading tastes, I knew nothing about him. His large stocky figure, greying leonine mane and piercing stare gave him an imperious look, but that was pure bluff. All he asked out of life was to be left alone.

They were a few years younger than Lalli and treated her with a mixture of awe and delicacy that I found endearing.

Ponni was the extrovert. She taught Carnatic music at our nearby college, but sang everything from Bollywood item numbers to hard rock. She dropped by occasionally and was easily persuaded to sing.

Lalli was awake. She had been crying. She made no attempt to check her tears now as she held out a hand. Frightened, and aching for comfort, I moved into her embrace. She held me close, her wiry arms light around me.

I felt curiously detached. I was as far away from tears as I would ever get. I had a job to do.

I pulled up a chair. Tearless now, her eyes held mine, prompting me to sternness.

'What is it, Lalli?' I asked.

Relief dawned, animating her face. Her eyes glimmered with hope. She took my hand in both hers and shut her eyes, overcome.

What had riven her so deeply that it disconnected her from life? I repeated my question, a little shocked at my daring, to breach a grief so intensely private. But somebody had to.

'I can't remember.' Her voice was barely a whisper, the first words she had spoken in three days.

She waited for her words to sink in.

What did she mean? Was she afraid of losing her mind? Had it happened already, the loss of name, face, place, erasures that cleared the slate for a new reality?

Lalli often railed against the growing epidemic of Alzheimer's Disease in the neighbourhood. She called it a diagnosis of expedience. It was not long before the diabolic Shantivan affair proved her right. It would be the cruellest irony if she had diagnosed the same illness in herself. If she had, she was wrong. But my conviction hardly counted. I was no neurologist.

Reading my thought, she smiled. 'It's not Alzheimer's.'

'What an idea! What kind of thing can't you remember? Names? Faces?'

'—terrible.'

'A case?'

'No! I—I *did* something terrible.'

The lost look had returned.

There was no getting around it. She must remember—or die.

'Help me,' she whispered. And then in sudden anguish her voice erupted, petulant like a child's. 'Sita, help me, I'm so tired, I can't bear it any more.'

The trembling frame was so slight in my arms.

'We'll remember it together, Lalli,' I said. 'Let's go find what you've forgotten.'

I meant that with every shred of purpose in my soul, but had no clue, none at all, where to begin.

She freed herself abruptly.

'Let's get some coffee, then.'

She followed me to the kitchen and sat down at the table. I got the coffee started, and cut a slice of the gingerbread I had baked yesterday.

'Tell me, Lalli.'

'I can't remember.'

I would have to smash a few of those barricades.

'You know what I'm asking, Lalli.'

'I don't want to remember. It's too terrible.'

'Omission or commission?' Always reliable, as the first link of the chain.

'Oh. Omission. One doesn't forget acts of commission.'

The words came quickly now. I poured the coffee and placed the cup before her. The intrusion irritated her.

She repeated, 'Telling a lie isn't irretrievable. But suppressing the truth—that's unforgiveable. How can I live with it!'

'You would never do that.'

'I did worse. I didn't see the truth. I didn't acknowledge the truth, and it's killing me. I don't know where to begin.'

'But I do.'

I waited till she stilled her trembling hands. 'I can't tell Savio, you understand, Sita? I can't tell Dr Q.'

I nodded.

Savio would find out quickly enough. He would take that act of omission, whatever it was, as his own burden, and run it down like the bloodhound he was, to the bare truth. It would destroy him.

Dr Q was out of the question. He would flounder in a morass of misery. That left only me.

'When did you realize this, Lalli?'

'When I was ill. Those two days when I was febrile, I was haunted by a memory that barely surfaced. The moment I focused on it, it disappeared. When the fever left me, I couldn't remember what it was.'

Exhausted with the effort, she sipped the coffee and took a hesitant nibble at the gingerbread.

'Too much cinnamon?'

'Just a touch. No orange?'

'Left it out this time.'

'One more slice, please. I can't trust my hands with that knife, not just yet.'

'Was it a face, a name, a place—'

'Was it a song? Or, a name in a song? I can't be sure even of that. It was music. Yes! Music!'

She sprang up, knocking over the cup, spattering hot coffee on her hands and mine, oblivious to everything but the sudden blaze of discovery that enlivened her.

'Music!'

The next instant, spark extinguished, she had subsided into silent anxiety. The note of music she had heard was lost. Fingers pressed against her mouth, eyes baffled, an effigy of torment, she challenged me with her utter stillness while I cleared up, and made fresh coffee. A faint lilt told me she was humming to herself, but her eyes still betrayed confusion.

Yet, her confusion couldn't possibly match my own predicament.

Music is my nemesis. Its teasing allure has baffled me all my life. I simply don't have it in me, and there is nothing I crave more. It would torment me less, were I tone deaf. Cruelly, I'm not. My brain rings with remembered notes I'm unable to either sing or replicate in imagination. Every word I write would be a note of music if it could.

If an elusive note of music was all that Lalli had to start with, how could I even hope to capture it for her?

Lalli certainly had an ear for music. I had no idea if she had the usual formal training as a child, but she had *kelvi gnanam*, literally auditory wisdom, and that's the most dependable understanding of all. She could spot the false note, every time.

I was defeated even before I started. Morosely, I turned my back on Lalli and fussed about on unnecessary tasks, unready to approach my cooling cup of coffee.

'Too rudimentary, Sita,' Lalli sighed. 'If only it were a simple word association like that.'

'What are you talking about?'

'What were you humming?'

I hadn't been—

Lalli sang a line, and I identified the buzz in my brain: *Jo achyutananda, jo jo mukunda…*

What possible association could this line of lullaby make?

Lalli held up my cup of coffee. 'Inhale.'

Tendrils of aroma teased me.

Kapi. *Not* coffee. Kapi.

Oh. *Kapi*!

'But Lalli, even if I was humming that, I had no idea the *raagam* was Kapi,' I protested.

Lalli laughed. 'You did, Sita, in some latent part of your consciousness.'

I revelled in her laugh, dismissing my inner musician, but pleased, just the same.

'I've been trying tricks of this sort for a fortnight, but it's far more complicated,' she sighed.

'Ponni asked if you'd like some music,' I blurted.

Lalli flushed. 'I've committed a crime. A crime I can't remember. A terrible crime.'

That seemed impossible, but I didn't want to contradict her.

I summoned up my nerve and went on, 'A crime to which the only clue is a note of music you can't remember. Ponni, the human iPod, is sure to have something useful in her.'

'No.'

'Right.'

The impasse lasted an hour.

Finally she sighed. 'You think I'm afraid Ponni might make me remember?'

'Yes.'

'And I may not be able to face the truth?'

It had to be said. 'Yes.'

Lalli laughed mirthlessly. 'Now you know why I asked for your help. Savio would never concede my cowardice.'

Neither could I, but I didn't argue.

'Tell Ponni to drop in any time she feels like a song.'

'Now?'

Lalli shrugged. What did we have to lose? It was a deadlock anyway.

As it happened, Ponni and Dr Q arrived together. I left Ponni chatting with Lalli and drew Dr Q into the kitchen. Lalli didn't seem to notice.

'She looks better,' he said encouragingly.

'She's trying to remember something.' This was as far as I was prepared to go.

'Oh?'

That was unanswerable.

He said, 'It might be dangerous. If she's forgotten it, she had very good reason to forget. It's dangerous.'

'We should stop her, then?'

He transfixed me with a look of deep irony. 'If we did, would it stop her?'

'But what if we refused to help her?'

'And so prolong her suffering? No, Sita. Do what she wants you to do.'

'How do you know—'

'You're the only one she'd ask. She knows my limitations. She's too protective of Savio. You're the only one with enough courage. You and—' His voice trailed off in confusion.

'Me, and who else, Dr Q?'

'She wouldn't want you to know.' His voice was bland but his eyes had turned lustrous with either anger or pain.

Ponni had chosen to sing an old film song. Her voice rose in saccharine anguish: *Meri beena tum bin roye*.

Dr Q ground his palms into his eyes. 'Two days ago, when I was really worried, I did ask her if I should send for—this other person. I did ask.'

'She said no?'

He nodded. 'I want you to know, I did ask.'

'Sure.'

'The blood tests are normal. Just get her to eat a little, and she'll be back.'

It was an empty assurance, neither of us believed it.

Ponni's song had ended. That *viraha geet* couldn't possibly have helped Lalli, but the choice was Ponni's.

I groaned when she began the next.

Dr Q raised his eyebrows. 'Don't like this song? Why? It's so beautiful.'

Beautiful, yes. But for me—loaded with angst.

It was the popular *Brochevarevarura* in zippy Khamas, the song that really defined my place in the family.

It floated out of the kitchen, most mornings. My mother, the only musical one, kept embroidering the *pallavi* ... till my father, working in his lab, heard her and stepped in with the *swaram*. Vasu would look up from whatever he was messing about with and belt out the mathematical progression. Neither of them sang well. The notes came by instinct, natural to their facility for numbers.

My mother's voice retreated, leaving them to argue it out in endless permutations and combinations that never, however wild, swerved from the melodic structure of the *raagam*. I, trapped in voiceless envy, even I could tell that.

Ponni seemed intent on unleashing all my demons this evening.

Next, she started on my father's favourite, *Chakkani rajamargamu*. He used Tyagaraja's emotional harangues very literally in educating us. The first two lines of this particular song had taken care of my early, and disastrous, driving lessons.[1]

Dr Q, in an enchanted daze by now, left the kitchen.

I followed.

Inspired by the audience, Ponni excelled herself. Usually her rich voice, so perfect in tone and modulation, kept itself carefully clear of emotion. Now she dropped her guard and the difference dazzled.

Dr Q clapped admiringly, and asked the name of the *raag*.

'Kharaharapriya.'

'*Karakara*priya,' Lalli amended with a laugh.

I wondered if Ponni would refute. She did, in a few words.

'Yes, of course, Ponni, Kharaharapriya is right. I'm very ignorant about these things,' Lalli said humbly.

But I was elated.

I had my first clue.

I couldn't wait to be rid of Ponni.

Lalli, though, seemed in no hurry.

She asked Ponni if she would sing a Dikshitar *kriti*. I knew Lalli's favourites, she often hummed a line or two.

---

1. When there's a royal and easy road ahead, why do you lose yourself in labyrinths, O my soul?

Muthuswami Dikshitar is the Shakespeare of music, and his myriad-minded compositions are definitely not meant to be sung by the faint of heart. They echo all the cultures on the planet, and can be delightfully antic, bewilderingly labyrinthine, majestic or tender.

My only brush with him was at the age of nine, when I was picked to sing an 'Indian song' in school.

'Not *too* Indian, dear,' Sister Rosemary warned.

Accordingly, I was coached in the lilting *Shyamale meenakshi,* which is based on an Irish air. I thought I had that right, but at the last moment, Vasu was pushed on stage alongside me.

'Your mum said it's a duet,' Sister frowned. 'Really, you should have warned us, Sita.'

Vasu, unperturbed, piped up in his high five-year-old voice.

After the first line, I could safely mime the rest, trusting him to carry the song through.

The memory distracted me, and I lost Ponni's reply.

She chose to sing *Yesterday* next, and followed that up with Billie Holiday's *Gloomy Sunday*.

Dr Q lost interest and gathered up the books he had brought Lalli.

Among them was Celine's *Journey to the End of Night*, a book Ramachandran had been yearning for. I said as much, and Ponni laughingly answered the book would be a suitable bribe if Lalli really wanted to hear a Dikshitar *kriti*.

I had no clue what she meant.

Later, Lalli filled me in. 'Ponni said after hearing Ramachandran sing a Dikshitar *kriti*, she never attempted one again, not even the simplest, not once in their forty years together. I could never have guessed that Ramachandran sings.'

I knew what she meant. When his wife sang, he glowed with pride but never betrayed that prescience of note or modulation, which is the unmistakable sign of a connoisseur.

'If he sings better than his wife, he must be worth hearing,' Dr Q decided, replacing the Celine on the table. 'Let me know when.'

It was an unusual gesture from Dr Q.

'So what have you discovered?' Lalli asked sharply as I shut the door on Dr Q.

'Karakarapriya.'

'Yes, that was foolish of me.'

'Foolish? It was the only bit of wisdom all evening.'

Our roles seemed reversed. She had no idea what I meant.

'Why did you make that pun?'

'Karakara' is the Tamil onamatopeia for crispness. So, who was Karakarapriya? The girl who loved crisp delights?

The word certainly narrowed the field.

This meant the language of Lalli's memory was Tamil.

Of course, it might also be the language of Lalli's *thought.*

We're all polyglot, but the intimacy of thought permits only one language. Which was it, with Lalli?

'A plump child,' Lalli said suddenly. 'Handful of murukku concealed in her blue pavadai.'

'She sang—Or, somebody around her sang Kharaharapriya—and you made up the pun? Was that the music you heard?'

'No.'

She hummed the *raagam.*

'Nothing like that. And, maybe, the child isn't from that memory at all.'

I heard her unsaid thought: it's not going to be this easy...

'Is there anything else, anything at all you remember?'

'I remember the crime.'

'The crime you committed? Then the matter's solved, Lalli.'

'Only the nature of the crime. The rest is a total blank.'

'So what was it? What was the crime you committed?'

'Murder.'

I stared at my aunt, shocked.

To Lalli, nothing is as sacred as human life. She has been battling the death penalty for years. She's hunted down the culprits in a dozen custodial deaths, long after those decorated officers were pensioned off into anonymity.

But of course, in the line of duty—

As usual, she uncannily read my thought. 'Killing in the line of duty is still murder, Sita. But mine was murder in the most criminal sense of the word. Of that I'm certain, or my guilt would not be so devastating. I can't remember whom I killed, how, when, why or where. The very fact that I've suppressed the memory tells me it's a crime too horrible to contemplate. And I must contemplate it, Sita, or my life has lost meaning.'

My aunt, the murderer.

She had abruptly switched sides now. Would the confession change her?

'You can't have committed murder,' I pointed out. 'You told me it was an act of omission.'

'It was still murder.'

And she walked away. That was the end of all conversation that day.

Late that night, I had two phone calls.

The first, surprisingly, was from Dr Q. 'Have you bribed him yet?'

It took a moment for the coin to drop.

'Oh, the Celine! No, not yet.'

'Do it tomorrow, please. Don't delay, Sita.'

'You think it's important, then?'

'Vital. You were distracted when she made the request, you didn't notice her eagerness.'

'First thing in the morning.'

The second call was Savio, of course.

He was held up, and wouldn't be able to make it to breakfast. After a hiatus he asked the dreaded question, 'How is she?'

I told him, very guardedly, she was trying to remember something—and finished with her request for a song from Ramachandran.

'You mean Ponni Mami.'

'No. Apparently he sings too. Did you know that?'

'No. Do you want me to ask him?'

'No, I'll do it.'

'Will you?'

A brittle silence stretched between us.

'Don't get like that, Sita,' Savio sighed. 'Just ask him, okay?'

'Okay.'

I was a little shocked by Savio's prescience. I *had* thought of putting it off. I enjoyed my occasional bookish sparrings with Ramachandran too much to call an end to them. And I knew, I just knew, once I had heard him sing we could no longer argue as equals. I would be in too much awe of him.

I was not in the slightest awe of Ponni. Music was a sound she produced with great felicity. It was only her voice I heard, not music. Not the secret language of notes that was always denied me. Ramachandran, I suspected, might understand it.

On the other hand, he might be an awful singer. His speaking voice was a breathy rasp. And, consoling myself he couldn't possibly produce anything more melodious than a rumble, I fell asleep.

It proved easier than I thought. I didn't even need the Celine. Ramachandran is a magnet for the neighbourhood's misguided youth and I was not surprised when his door was opened by a tattooed kid flashing nuts, bolts and screws on most moveable parts—

I counted four separate piercings over the eyebrows alone.

'Come in, Sita. Back to work, Rocky.'

Rocky shot me a belligerent look and slunk back to his books.

I followed Ramachandran into the living room.

The vestibule, where Rocky now laboured, was wrongly named. It was the largest room in the house, cheerfully sunlit, bright with cushions and furniture meant to loll in.

Kids dropped in to study, or just be. Ramachandran didn't talk much. They hung around when Ponni sang, and sometimes joined in. Mostly, they read, ate, and left, but the effect was usually therapeutic.

'Can you believe it? His name actually is Rocky,' Ramachandran marvelled in an undertone. 'But then again—why not? I was expecting you, Sita. Ponni said Lalli would like to hear some Dikshitar *kritis*.'

'Yes. Could you—'

'Of course. Any time she wants.'

Quick and painless, but I wasn't done yet. Ramachandran raised an eyebrow.

I showed him the book. 'It's Dr Q's.'

His outstretched hand retreated. I could almost see his thought in words: *why this generosity from a stranger?*

'Dr Q will be here this evening, say around six.'

Dr Q changed from stranger to rasikan, absorbed unquestioningly into a musician's extended family. 'Six is fine with me, but will that suit Lalli? Ponni has a class at six, so it'll be just me.'

'She'll risk it.'

That behind us, we settled down with P.G.Wodehouse, lamenting his recent resurrection by Sebastian Faulks.

'Such efforts always remind me of that dreadful Poe short story.'

I laughed. I knew the one he meant. *The Facts in the Case of M.Valdemar,* in which a corpse is resurrected—very briefly—with a surge of galvanic current. The description of the crisis was unforgettable.

'*No person had as yet been mesmerized* in articulo mortis,' Ramchandran quoted happily. 'If you like your marrow frozen, there's no one like Edgar Allan Poe.'

'Yeah, he's really creepy,' Rocky agreed enthusiastically. '*As of someone gently rapping, rapping at my chamber door.*'

Ramachandran's face mirrored my surprise.

'Accha? So you've read *The Raven*?' he asked casually.

'Read? He's on YouTube. Spooked me. Must've watched it like a million times.'

Darn. Now Poe would have the face of John Cusack for evermore.

'What about you, Sita, do you sing?' Ramachandran asked suddenly.

I shook my head and made a quick exit.

Lalli awaited Ramachandran with visible impatience.

I could feel her straining to capture that elusive note all morning.

In an effort to distract her I asked, 'What kind of murukku did she hide in her skirt? That plump little Karakarapriya?'

'Kai murukku,' she answered at once. 'Small homemade ones, but so delicious, I can still taste them.'

Startled by her words, she shook her head in incomprehension. 'You caught me off guard there, Sita. Yes, but I can't remember the provenance of that memory—where is that memory from? Who was this plump child? Who called her Karakarapriya?'

'Was it you, Lalli? Perhaps it's a memory from your childhood.'

'Oh, I was not a karakarapriyai, I craved sweets! And I didn't have a blue pavadai, I always wanted one, a Mayil-kazhuthu.'

Peacock's neck, the wonderful blue-green shot silk of Kanjivaram.

'You have a sari, though,' I laughed.

'My mother's gift, when I joined the police. No, that plump kid wasn't me. But the taste of that murukku is still with me.'

'Describe it.'

She shut her eyes for a long moment.

'Small. Four circles, not more. Beautifully twirled, small precise twists. A lovely pale gold. A faint aroma of coconut. No cumin or sesame, just a hint of asafoetida, and the nutty scent of roasted rice.'

Her eyes were still shut, and I was glad she couldn't see my disappointment. I knew where that memory came from. It was recent—too recent.

But how old was her crime?

Hesitantly I asked, 'Do you have a sense of how old you were when—'

'I committed murder? I do, though I can't say why. Older than you. Mid-forties, probably, my most crowded years. I was here, there, everywhere. It all went in a flash. Perhaps that's why I suppressed the memory.'

'But why remember it now?'

'I told you. The fever brought it up.'

Why was I unconvinced by that explanation? There was no time to question that now. Dr Q arrived, and soon after, Ramachandran.

Pristine in crisp veshti and bush shirt, his dark

face lit with a broad stripe of vibhuti, Ramachandran looked of the earth earthly, an unlikely candidate for any kind of musical transcendence.

Relief made me voluble, and it was some time before we got down to music.

Ramachandran had brought a book. He laid it down, a little shyly, next to the Celine.

Dr Q picked it up eagerly. 'Huysmans!' Joris-Karl Huysmans, the nineteenth-century French novelist, was a writer both Dr Q and I loved.

Ramachandran bowed. 'A fair exchange.'

'Not really. I will be in your debt by the end of the evening.' Dr Q produced a small notebook. 'I have the names, written down, of the *raags* we heard yesterday. Khamas and Kharaharapriya.'

I intervened. 'Lalli, which song do you have in mind?'

'Any Dikshitar *kriti* will do.'

I wondered how she could be so vague.

'Dikshitar didn't compose anything in Kharaharapriya,' Ramachandran surprised me by saying.

'But he wrote hundreds—'

'Five hundred, maybe more. But no Kharaharapriya. Khamas, then.'

Dr Q looked around a little wildly. 'Don't you need some accompaniment? Tamboor, harmonium?'

'Or a little black box with flashing lights? I leave all that to Ponni. A capella, me.'

He hummed and looked a question at Lalli. She nodded brightly.

The first notes of *alapanai* glided out contemplatively, in growing accents of wonder, almost as if he couldn't believe his luck. The breathy rasp was now a meditative vibrato, leaving the faintest space for thought between each note.

His voice became an instrument of touch, examining with infinite delicacy the texture of that invisible idea he held. What was it? How did it land here, within his ambit? He asked the question over and over again, almost, but not entirely convinced that this miraculous moment was his. And then, as his conviction grew to a certainty, his voice rose in jubilant paean.

I wished I knew what he saw, what it was that he revelled in. His voice had converted the tease in Khamas to pure indulgence, tenderness and delight.

And then, the first line of the *pallavi* explained it. *Shri Swaminathaya Namaste…*

It was a long time since I had heard music of such beauty. His voice almost dandled the notes. I say almost, because it still had a reserve of awe.

As the tempo hastened that humility melted away, the notes became energetically declarative, rising to a crescendo of pure delight, and then falling away into tenderness, but now with the assurance of utter belonging.

It was a very long journey to have travelled in less than ten minutes.

I looked around.

Dr Q had his eyes shut, his hands in an attitude of prayer. His features looked unfamiliar, the deeply etched lines erased.

Lalli, on the other hand, was calm, unmoved.

'So is that Khamas enough for you?' Ramachandran smiled.

'Yesterday this *raag* was flamboyant. Today it is mystic,' Dr Q said.

'I don't know about mystic, I'm not a religious man,' Ramachandran replied. 'Truth be told, I don't think Dikshitar was, either.'

'Not religious? I can't believe that.' Out came the notebook again and I realized Dr Q had gone Wikipedia on us. 'I have a list. All his compositions classified by deity, different kshetra—temples, that is. He could only have composed in religious ecstasy. And you? Vibhuti shining on your forehead, what is that?'

Ramachandran laughed. 'Tell me, sir, has a child ever whispered a secret in your ear?'

Taken aback, Dr Q hesitated before nodding.

'What are your emotions at that moment? Delight? Wonder, that you have been chosen as confidante? And, a sudden dazzling glimpse of the world as the child sees it? Is that not revelation enough? In the legend, Kartikeya whispers in his father's ear the word that is the essence of the universe, and so becomes Swaminatha, the Lord's own Lord.

Think of Shiva's moment—could it not have been Dikshitar's too? Certainly, his poetry is full of gods and goddesses, but what are these but human experience? All his compositions are expressions of wonder over the beauty of this experience, but it takes a lifetime to understand them. At sixty-three, I haven't even begun.'

Dr Q popped the notebook in his pachydermatous bag. Except for that bag, the man was neat as a cat.

'One more?' Lalli hesitated. 'Or do I ask too much?'

'I'll sing till you beg me to shut up. Oh, about the vibhuti I wear—Lalli, this might interest you. A year ago, on Ganesh Chathurthi, a young man rang my doorbell. Ponni opened the door, and the next moment, I heard her scream. I rushed there to find our visitor had toppled over in an epileptic fit. It must have lasted about five minutes. When he revived, he told me he had this complaint since childhood. His father was known for his Harikatha—the art form where the story of the Lord is told through music, song and drama—and this boy too sang along with him. I don't know who sent him to me, but he brought me vibhuti in a *panneer* leaf, from Pazhani. I asked him to sing and he sang a verse or two of Thirupugazh so beautifully, I was moved to tears. Since then he's been a constant visitor. I don't know much about him, but I would like to make certain he gets treatment for his fits. So far, his father has been his only doctor, gives him some rubbish and makes him pray. Could you recommend someone? They're poor and can't afford much.'

'Send him to me, and I'll fix him up with a neurologist,' Dr Q said.

'Thank you, I will bring him to you. But my story isn't over. One afternoon, when he came in, I was humming and he stopped me saying, "Please don't sing that, or I'll have a fit." I told him not to be ridiculous, and there was only one way to prove him wrong. I sat him down and sang the song. I had just got past the *pallavi* when he erupted in convulsions. This was no pretense, I assure you, the fits were genuine. He was unconscious for half an hour. I persuaded him to stay, but he wouldn't agree. It ended with me taking him home.'

'Will you sing that song for us now?' Lalli asked.

'Certainly, if you wish.'

He sang an elegant *Mohanam* with such deceptive ease, it was only the bravura verse with the signature mudra, *Guruguha*, that betrayed it was Dikshitar's *kriti*.

'What is it you're waiting to hear?' he asked Lalli. 'I see it's no particular *kriti* or *raagam*. You're looking for something, aren't you?'

Lalli hesitated. 'I'm trying to remember something,' she admitted. 'It's a passage which, I think, might be a Dikshitar *kriti*, because of the abrupt shifts in scale. But that's all I can tell. I'll know when I hear it.'

'Then let me see if I can open a few windows,' Ramachandran said.

He launched into an *alapanai* that sent notes spinning in regression. I didn't recognize the *raagam*, I just went with it. It didn't open windows, it pushed open doors, broke down walls, drew the eye beyond the horizon to a far point so distant it could only topple into melancholy. But the *pallavi* opened on a playful, almost antic note, quickly progressing to a tender recollection of beauty, poignant, but untainted by loss. As he developed the *pallavi*, Ramachandran's voice almost swooned with tenderness on the last phrase—*gaana lole, susheele baale.* Once more he approached the phrase with a delicacy almost evanescent—

Lalli's cry shattered the air. It was wordless, discordant, enraged. She sprang up, clutching the table for support, and leaned forward urgently, eyes staring at nothing.

In the silence I thought I heard our hearts beat. *Thud, thud, thud, thud.*

Thud, thud, thud, thud.

Someone was knocking on the door.

To my surprise, it was Savio.

'What's wrong with the doorbell, didn't it ring?' he frowned.

We hadn't heard it.

'Ramachandran here? Right. Step aside, Sita.'

I caught a glimpse of the room before Savio

entered. It was still frozen in a tableau of shock. Ramachandran's lips, arrested in that last phrase were still parted to enunciate the next syllable.

Dr Q, his hand extended towards Lalli's, had stopped midway.

This was a Savio I hadn't met before. He annihilated us with a stony glare and addressed Ramachandran.

'Mr Ramachandran, we would like to talk with you urgently. Please come with me to the chowki. The jeep's waiting.'

Ramachandran, baffled, stared at Savio.

'Please, sir. Don't make it difficult for me,' Savio looked away.

With a bellow of rage, Ramachandran lunged forward. Savio caught his arm. Ramachandran looked helplessly at Lalli, but made no attempt to shake free.

'May I speak with my wife, please?'

'Later. Sita will convey your message'

'Are you arresting me?'

'Not yet. It will be easier to talk at the chowki.'

'What is it, Savio?' Lalli asked, almost in a whisper.

The question was pointless. Savio did not answer, except with glance of heavy patience.

All of us knew, all too well, the crisis that had transformed Savio.

It could only be—murder.

I watched Ramachandran collect himself into a semblance of his usual dignity.

He looked a question at Lalli.

'Please go with Savio, Ramachandran.' Lalli's voice was colder than ice.

'I'll come with you.' Dr Q picked up his bag.

'I don't think so, Dr Q,' Savio said gently.

'You have your thought, and I have mine. Let's go.'

Lalli said, 'I wish Dr Q weren't mixed up in this.'

'What is this, Lalli?' I demanded. 'Was the whole evening a set up? Did you lure Ramachandran here for this?'

She flushed angrily. 'Even murderers don't sink so low, Sita.'

I apologized, but I was furious. I couldn't bear the thought of having been part of this. I left the room.

I heard the phone ring in the living room. Lalli picked it up.

A little later, she walked into my room and sat down on the bed, exhausted.

I will never forget her face at that moment. It looked as if it was cast in bell metal. It had the roseate patina of an old lamp, just recently doused. Like that lamp, the sheen retreated from her skin as I looked, the story on pause until somebody thought to light it again. Her eyes glittered in deep wells of lamp black, her mouth a ridge of bitterness.

'We can quarrel later, Sita. That was Savio on the phone. A musician called Subbu Bhagavathar was murdered this afternoon—'

'The vibhuti boy's father!' I burst out. What made me so certain?

'It appears so. The boy, Senthil Kumaran, has confessed to the murder. He's made a statement saying he murdered his father under the direction of Ramachandran, who is his true father.'

'What!'

'He made the statement in what Shukla calls drama Tamil, so he got his buddy Shaktivel to translate.'

'Shukla's back?'

'Evidently. Savio suspects Shaktivel has got it all wrong and wants me to sit in with Shukla. They're in Sion.'

'Let's go. Lalli, what about Ponni?'

Lalli shook her head. 'Let's not waste time, Sita. Savio will manage that.'

Ten minutes later we had hit the highway. At Santa Cruz I turned into the newly opened freeway. Even if it meant backtracking, it would be quicker than the road through Dharavi.

I stole a look at Lalli as I drove. She was as remote from the moment as she had been at that electric moment when she had interrupted Ramachandran's song.

I was certain she had that elusive note now, and perhaps the memory had followed immediately.

I didn't think Shaktivel was dependable as an interpreter. He was Shukla's protégé, and I couldn't think of a more disastrous combination.

That reminded me I had yet to tell Lalli about Ambarnath—

Just then the exit appeared, and I forgot all about it.

Hurtling through a wormhole must feel very much like this, I thought. Nothing could possibly connect the grisly murder we were travelling towards with the one Lalli had left behind. Yet the evening now seemed a shining line of silk stretched taut between them. The murder behind us had disrupted the world as I had known it for the last few years.

And in case this is our first meeting, let me assure you our menage at 44, Utkrusha-B, Vile Parle East, is by no means a calm place. Mayhem has its finger pressed down on the doorbell most days. Corpses come calling. People disappear. Hearts break. Lives mend.

And there are our own fears, hopes and impossible dreams.

Savio, these days is a divided man. He must, but cannot leave the police. Shukla, who will never leave, fiercely cultivates irony as defence. Gallows humour is his stock in trade. Dr Q, police surgeon, more appropriately high priest of the dead, brings home grisly bits to spar over with my aunt and enjoys talking books with me.

And I? My presence here is purely accidental. I had never known murder outside a book when I first met Lalli. It took me months to learn the L.R. scrawled on the files that arrived every week stood for Last Resort. And it wasn't till I opened one of them by accident, spilling a bunch of gruesome photographs, that I realized they came from Homicide. I've travelled light years since then. Between murder and mayhem, I write.

And all this coheres as life solely because of my aunt.

Between the murder we were hurtling towards, and the one Lalli had forgotten, stretched this shining thread of our lives together, and I could not bear for it to snap.

Taanam

Shukla was waiting for us at the gate. I hadn't seen him since March when I had tagged along with him to Ambarnath. Shukla's dazzling ivorine smile switched off abruptly when he caught sight of Lalli. He quickly composed his features, but not before I had caught a glimpse of fear.

'So, Sita, you came by freeway? I warned Traffic guys well in advance. Lalli, I told Savio we can wait till morning, but—' he grimaced apologetically. 'Savio said this Ramchandar is singing lady's husband. Same one he sends boys to, or another one?'

'Singing lady has only one husband,' I pointed out.

'Then there is definite blackness in dal. Shaktivel is here, he will tell you.'

Shaktivel stepped up and saluted Lalli smartly.

'Let's hear the story, Shaktivel,' Lalli said.

'I have prepared chamber,' Shukla announced, steering Lalli away from the large, brightly lit hall. 'Too much roughriffs everywhere.'

Shaktivel threw open a door, switched on the lights. An ancient AC roared awake, yawning a hot fetid exhalation.

'Rat,' Shaktivel suggested. Before we could stop him, he had leaped at the window. Shukla, with quick reflexes, switched off the roar. Shaktivel tugged off the AC cover and plunged his arm into the dark maw.'Ow!' Something had Shaktivel in its grip and would not let go. His arm was stuck.

'Idiot!' Shukla growled, grabbing Shaktivel by the collar and yanking him in an attempt to extract his arm whole. It emerged after three tries, with enraged rat attached.

Lalli picked up the paperweight on the table and hurled it at the rat. Shaktivel stared in amazement as the glass sphere homed in on the rat's skull with a splat.

'Get cleaned up, get your shots and return in ten minutes, I'll be waiting on the porch,' Lalli said wearily, and left the room.

'Is she ill?' Shukla asked in an undertone.

'Yes.'

'Looks serious. Why didn't you tell me, Sita?'

That reproach was the last straw. Hot tears stung my face.

'I've not seen Savio, but even he thinks Shukla is dead. Theek hai, I will go to source, direct Gangotri.'

And before I could stop him, he had stalked off to find Lalli.

To my surprise, Lalli stalled Shukla's questions by saying, 'Shukla, I was about to ask you to join Sita in helping me when this case turned up. And no, I'm not ill. I have a problem to solve.'

'Personal?'

'Very personal.'

'Shukla is with you 24/7. This case is safe with Shaktivel. He is brilliant.'

'Are you mad, Shukla? He's an idiot,' I burst out again.

'As usual, Sita, you are hitting nails. The boy is brilliant, but he has no brain. Just now we are beholding same. Since we are now co-working on Lalli's matter, better we dentate right now.'

'Dentate?'

'You are writer, but not reading. Front page is always dentating in international politics.'

'Have you interrogated this boy yet, Shukla?' Lalli broke into Shukla's short course in semantics.

'Lalli, he is only talking drama in Tamil. If you ask me, insanity.'

'What do you mean, talking drama?'

Shukla turned to me helplessly. 'Like in Ambarnath?'

'Oh!' Light, most welcome and forgiving, lifted my despair.

'Lalli, the boy must have been reciting Tevaram.'

The Tevaram forms a devotional core of Tamil poetry. It reflects the intimacy between the speaker and the Absolute in the form of Shiva.

Shukla's 'drama' referred to the recitation we had heard at Ambarnath.

'No, no,' Shukla refuted this urgently. 'That was religious. This is opposite.'

Shaktivel, bandaged and in mufti, hurried up to us. 'Sorry, sir, no uniform available.'

He was wearing a T-shirt with a restaurant logo. I imagined he had menaced a passing canteen boy and ripped it off his back. That seemed his brand of heroics.

'What did Senthil tell you?' Lalli asked him in Tamil.

He answered her first in English, then in Marathi, then in Hindi, and finally in a mixture of all three with a stray Tamil word thrown in.

'What language do you speak at home?' Lalli asked.

'Same to same, madam. Mixed.'

'Did you understand Senthil's language?'

'Nothing to understand. He was shouting, "Father! Father!"'

'What was the word he used?'

'Pita! Pita!'

'Pita?' The last word I would have expected from Senthil.

'*Mata pita guru deivam*,' Shukla explained helpfully. 'You are not knowing Sanskrit, I think, Sita.'

'Shaktivel, think for a moment before you answer my question,' Lalli continued. 'Did he say *Pita* or *Pitta*?'

Shaktivel and Shukla consulted over this. 'Pitta. Yes definitely Pitta,' Shukla said. 'What it means, Lalli?'

'Madman.'

'He was calling us mad? With Pitta he said another word like ... piri ... piri,' Shukla said.

'Pitta, *piraichoodi*?'

'That's it!'

Pitta, piraichoodi perumaane—Lunatic! Crescent-crowned Lord! That is how the poet Sundarar addresses Shiva.

But why would a man who has murdered his father erupt into poetry?

'What happened next?' Lalli asked.

'He kept shouting, calling for his father. Not Pitta now—*Appane, appane*, like that. So I told him his father was dead. That's when he said that's not my father. Then who is, I asked. He is, he said. *Ivan alla, avan. Yeh nahin, woh*. Like that. *Appan alla aayan*, something like that, I did not understand. *Appan alla, aayan*. What is aayan, I asked. Give me name, I said. Write down name and address, telephone number, landline, mobile. He started laughing. My father has no telephone, he said. No name, no address. He made me do this, now he's not talking to me.'

'You were there too, Shukla, you heard all this?'

'Yes, but he spoke only in Tamil.'

'So, Shaktivel, what next?'

'I asked him why he killed his father. Again he said, "Appan alla, aayan". Why did you kill him? I asked. And he answered, "I obeyed my father's orders". Like that it went on for nearly one hour, round and round. Then he says, "I'm feeling sleepy, now I will go to sleep."'

'He was still in his blood-soaked clothes, hands, face, all covered with his father's blood and he was ready to fall asleep!' Shukla's voice shook with horror. 'If this is not madness, what do you call it, Lalli?'

'I haven't seen the boy yet, Shukla. So what happened, Shaktivel, did he fall asleep?'

'I told him he can't sleep till he gives us a name. And so he did. He gave us name and address of one Ramachandran, 54, Utkrusha—'

'Yes, we know the address,' Shukla snapped. 'Get on with what happened after that.'

'Is this your father's name, I asked. He answered with a question: are you asking about my real father or the dead man? Your real father, I told him. Then he got cheeky. He said, "You have his name, you have his address, why don't you ask him?" And then he fell asleep. Just like that he toppled over, fast asleep.'

'Nervous exhaustion,' Shukla said carefully.

'Is he awake now?' Lalli asked.

'We can wake him up.' Shaktivel had an evil grin.

'No. You'll do no such thing. I'd like to see him, though.'

Shukla led us to the holding cell.

Senthil was asleep on the floor, handcuffed and chained. That seemed a needless amount of restraint.

'He killed his father,' Shukla said. 'His *father*.'

Italicizing it, in case we hadn't noticed the patricide.

Shukla's voice startled the sleeping boy. He sat up, then tried to rise, only to fall back defeated by his chains.

A frightened cry broke from him, its note changing to horror as he tried to pluck the bloody clothes from his body. This was no longer a murderer, just a bewildered young man trapped in a huddle of bloodstained clothing.

'Appa! Appa! Where are you? What's happening?' he shouted. 'Where am I? Why am I bleeding? Where have you brought me?'

As yet he hadn't noticed us. He was in a torment of urgency, trying to free himself.

Lalli called out in Tamil, 'Who are you?'

At that he froze.

His eyes focused on us in slow deliberation.

He folded his hands in plea.

'Amma, you speak Tamil, you can understand me. Please call my father. Where is he? Where has he left me? Is this a hospital? No, it can't be! I must be very sick, I'm bleeding everywhere. Call my father, before I die, I beg of you.'

The words he used were *paithiya aspithri*—mental hospital.

'What is your name?' Lalli asked again.

'Senthil. Senthil Kumaran. My father's name is

Subramanya Bhagavathar. He must have written down the address in your register. Has he gone out to get something to eat? How long have I been asleep?'

'How long do you usually sleep?'

'They say about two or three hours. Sometimes my father gives me medicine that makes me sleep longer.'

'Tablets?'

'No. Not English medicine. He gives me a kashayam that relieves my headache.'

'Does your head ache now?'

'Terribly!' And he began crying, wringing his hands, his voice an infantile sob, 'Appa! Appa!'

'Your Appa is dead!' Shaktivel said. 'You killed him.'

Senthil stopped wailing. His face passed from misery to anger. 'What did you say?'

'I said your father is dead. You killed him,' Shaktivel repeated.

I was surprised Shukla made no protest at his talking out of turn.

'Please don't say such bad things,' Senthil said with a shudder. 'My father is a good man, don't wish him ill.' He turned to Lalli. 'Amma, why does this man talk to me like that? Why am I chained like an animal? You didn't do this to me last time. Is this a different hospital?'

'Do you know the name of the hospital you were in earlier?' Lalli asked.

'Yes. At first I was in Sion Hospital. They gave me shocks. I became like stone. Then they put me in Thana Mental Hospital. I was there for six months. They didn't chain me like this.'

'Senthil, you are not in hospital now,' Lalli said. 'You're in jail.'

'Jail! Why? Did the police bring me in from the road? Had I fallen there? Does my father know I'm here?'

'Your father is dead, Senthil.'

An animal howl broke from him. It tore past him and went echoing down the narrow corridor.

I turned and ran, nausea lurching up my ribs. I went out of the building.

The night air, thick as it was with the noise and stench of traffic, still held some semblance of life. I drank it in, trying to fill the vacuum within my skull.

'Sita, are you okay?' Shukla manifested in the gloom. 'Lalli wants you back in there. Here. Drink this.' He had brought a glass of water from the cooler.

It made my nausea retreat. 'Shukla, that boy's completely clueless. He doesn't know about the murder.'

'He could be fooling us.' But he sounded doubtful. 'Lalli's asked for him to be taken into chamber.'

'Rat chamber?'

'No.' Shukla's teeth shone in the dark. 'For you

we are having one with cat. Cat chamber is for viewing rat chamber. Wired up.'

Lalli had talked with him some more, then insisted on a wash and a change of clothing for the prisoner. Forensics had collected all the samples they wanted off him, and the clothes could be sent to them.

I joined Lalli in the cat chamber. There actually was a cat, an animal of some discernment and intelligence, judging by the way she snarled at Shaktivel from her perch on a cupboard.

Lalli met me with an enquiring look. Shaktivel ostentatiously dusted a chair for me and set down a glass of water with the greatest delicacy as if it might shatter on contact with the table. Lalli seemed to have got him tongue-tied.

'Shukla, please sit down. Let me summarize what the boy has said so far. First, he did not recognize his surroundings.

'Second, he has no memory of recent events—his last memory is having lunch in the temple just before eleven-thirty. He left the temple immediately after lunch.

'Third, he last saw his father this morning at about ten when he left home on his rounds to distribute vibhuti and collect contributions for the Harikatha. This, he says, has been the routine all this month. If his route is near the temple, he stops by. If there's any food, the priests generally ask him to eat there.

'Fourth, he was confined to the Thana mental asylum last year. He was discharged against medical advice. His father took him home on request.

'Fifth, he's been subject to epileptic fits ever since he can remember. He can never recall the period between convulsions and waking up.

'Sixth, he has never committed any act of violence during these seizures. He expressed total disbelief over the news of his father's death.

'Seventh, and my last point, he insisted the blood on his clothing was his own. When I asked him to point out his injuries, he was taken aback. He then said he had no idea where the blood came from. These facts apart, he seems well oriented.

'Now I propose to show him Shaktivel's photographs.'

Shaktivel came forward purposefully, mobile in hand. Shukla intercepted him and produced an iPad, intent on enhancing the horror of the crime scene.

The victim, who appeared to be in his early sixties, had been attacked with a blunt instrument. He lay face down in a pool of blood, the back of his head a pulpy mess of brain and shattered bone. So extensive was the injury that the skull seemed to have exploded. The spatter of blood and brain covered a fairly wide perimeter. That couldn't have happened unless the assailant had struck repeatedly.

The weapon had been flung down next to the body.

It was an iron pestle, such as is common in an old-fashioned kitchen. We have one at home, usually used to crack open coconuts. I only recognized this one from the familiar shape of the grip. Its broad end was obscured, coated with blood and webbed with shredded membrane and pulped brain.

Finally, there was a picture of the victim's face, photographed after the body had been shifted. The features were curiously composed, as if a death mask of tranquility had been carefully fitted over the chaos.

Senthil had been photographed too. His outstretched hands were bloody, his clothes soaked, his face spattered with blood. Yet his eyes regarded the camera with a calm defiance. I shuddered as I imagined the faint hint of a smile.

Senthil was brought in, escorted by two towering constables. He was still handcuffed. Jail couture had transformed him. His wet hair was slicked back, and that, along with the ear studs and designer stubble, gave his thin face a very trendy look. I realized now he was older than I had imagined, perhaps twenty-five or so. He was trembling visibly, either from fear or physical exhaustion.

Lalli asked the two constables to leave. Then, wordlessly, she displayed the iPad.

The dead man stared at Senthil, calm beneath his halo of gore.

'Chittappa!' Senthil's whisper of anguish turned my spine to ice.

He had identified the dead man not as his father, but as his father's younger brother, Chittappa, his *uncle*. He kept whispering the word in mounting horror. Then he buried his face in his hands with a groan.

'What happened to him? What happened to my uncle?'

The question came in a very controlled voice. For the first time I heard the sane tone of twenty-five.

'This.'

Lalli showed him the picture of the body lying with the skull stowed in, followed by a close-up of the bloody pestle.

'Who did this to my uncle?'

The calmness was gone. The veins on his temples bunched up engorged as he shouted angrily, pounding the table with his steel restraints.

Lalli showed him the last picture in which he faced the camera holding out his bloody hands.

'I saw this? I was there? Wait—you're not saying I did it? Are you accusing me of killing my uncle? Is that why you have me in chains?'

'Yes.'

'You told us you killed him,' Shaktivel butted in.

'No. No. No!'

It was some time before he spoke again.

'I don't remember being there. I may have

wandered there. I often walk after a fit until I fall asleep. Sometimes I sleepwalk. I don't remember anything of that. But even if I had wandered, I could never have hurt him.'

Lalli said quietly. 'You were there next to the body very soon after he was killed. You were holding that pestle when the police found you. Did you kill this man? Isn't this man your father?'

'My father! How can a son kill his own father? Oh, the very thought is evil—how can you even say it aloud? This man is not my father. He's my Chittappa, my father's younger brother. Who took these pictures? All these pictures lie.'

'These photographs don't lie, Senthil. These facts are true. A neighbour called the police.'

'Then, Police Amma, I'll tell you something. The neighbours all think I'm mad, but I'm not. I only get fits. Where is my father? You must find him first. And then, listen, Amma, I can call this gentleman I know. He is a big man. Educated, not like my father. He will explain all about me. He won't mind talking to you—but, I don't know. Oh! If he hears you have arrested me, maybe he won't have anything to do with me. Oh, what will I do then?' His voice turned into a wail.

'Give me his name. Do you have an address?'

'Ramachandran Mama, that is Ramachandran, I don't know his initials. His address—oh, I have his card in my pants pocket, but you took away my clothes—'

'Is it 54, Utkrusha—

'Azad Road, Vile Parle, yes! How do you know? Do you know him?'

'Perhaps, I'm not sure.'

'Please talk to him, Amma. Tell him I am here. No, I don't care if he disowns me now, all I want is for you to know what he thinks of me, what he knows of me. That will suffice.'

'I will do that. Senthil, I will ask you one more time: Did you kill this man?'

'No!'

'I'm calling Savio to send Ramchandran here,' Shukla said, sotto voce.

'No. Sita will fetch him.'

I hesitated.

'Please, Sita,' Lalli's eyes held fear, not command. She couldn't possibly think I'd refuse—No, her fear had nothing to do with the request. It had something to do with this young man before us.

I was certain of that, somehow. Lalli was not horrified by Senthil, or the crime he had committed, but she was afraid of him. He had brought back a memory that terrified her.

All the way on that tense drive to Vile Parle, all I could think about was this.

Savio's dramatic interruption had distracted me from the true purpose of this evening. Perhaps its purpose had been achieved, after all.

Distracted by Ramachandran's crisis, I had ignored Lalli's. Now I tried to recall the moment when she had cried out.

Surely it was a cry of discovery—no, it was a cry of alarm. Her eyes had the same look of fear I had noticed a few minutes ago.

I tried recalling the phrase, almost evanescent in its tenderness: *gaana lole, susheele baale*.[2]

As usual, my brain refused to humour my straining soul. The music slid in my blood like an entrapped bubble of air, too paltry to nourish, not large enough to kill.

It had been lethal enough to threaten Lalli. What did it mean to her?

My own pulse raced as if I felt her fear. No, this was no transference. I was afraid, frightened by Lalli's fear.

Never before had I seen her afraid.

Three years ago when the Rassiwala murders dogged us, Lalli had been disturbed, but never frightened.

A few months back the horrific crimes at Kandewadi had left her withdrawn, revolted by the unimaginable evil, but she had confronted it without fear.

Now she flinched from confrontation. Her loss of memory was willful protection against a truth too

2. O beautiful song, my virtuous one, my child.

terrible to be borne. What if she had in actual fact committed murder? How would she live with it?

How would *I* live with it?

Savio greeted me with an unexpected hug, taking the crowding questions right out of my mind. So Ramachandran had been cleared. Relief was written all over Savio. He blamed Shaktivel's idiocy for giving him the worst half hour of his life.

'Until Lalli phoned me with the facts, I was going nuts, just sitting in silence with Ramachandran glowering at me. Heck, I'd nearly arrested him. I couldn't have borne it.'

I finished the thought—Savio couldn't have borne it if Ramachandran were guilty.

He had great respect for the way Ramachandran dealt with 'lost kids' as he called them. The influence Ramachandran's kindness had on them was undeniable. And that, I knew, had informed Savio's brutal attack on Ramachandran. What if Senthil were one of those lost kids? Had Ramachandran led him into crime? A crime so heinous it didn't bear thinking about? Had he, also, depraved the kids Savio had entrusted to his care? That thought, almost as heinous as the crime itself, had terrified Savio.

'Lalli called. She wants to confront Ramachandran with the boy,' Savio said uncomfortably. 'I don't think it's a good idea.'

'Why not?'

'From what Lalli says, the boy's very unstable. Perhaps he should be allowed to rest a little before we question him. If there's any truth in his earlier ravings, the sight of Ramachandran might send him nuts again—but then perhaps that's just what Lalli wants to see.'

'Wouldn't you?'

'Yeah, but not in the chowki.'

Savio is fascinated by the neuroscience of crime. A year ago he had set up a lab with a couple of friends, and they were testing out software they had developed for interrogation. They had no funding and, as a result, Savio was usually running on empty. If it worked, it would be a breakthrough, taking brain fingerprinting several notches higher. It all seemed very H.G. Wells to me. Funny how the older brand of science fiction matches up more easily with new inventions. Savio was itching to get Senthil into his Truth Machine.

Dr Q came out with Ramachandran.

I watched Ramachandran extend a hesitant hand.

Dr Q, who generally shrinks from physical contact, embraced him and walked quickly away to his car.

Ramchandran stood watching him thoughtfully, then turned to us.

'Good of you to come, Sita,' he said.

'Do you feel up to talking to the boy now?' Savio asked.

'Oh, it hasn't been Guantanamo. Not yet, anyway,' Ramachandran answered wryly as he followed me.

He was silent all the way. I was worried about how much to tell him if he started questioning me about Senthil, but he said nothing at all. Only once did he break the silence to say, 'I hope this isn't too much of a strain on Lalli.' He didn't continue, although I sensed he was on the verge of alluding to the moment when she had interrupted his song.

Neither did I say anything about it. I merely asked him if he had spoken with his wife, to which he nodded silently.

The song Lalli had interrupted resonated in the silence, wildly inappropriate to our errand, the notes escalating and plummeting like the desperate flapping of a trapped bird.

Lalli interviewed Ramachandran in the cat chamber—Senthil had been taken back to his cell.

She began by asking him what he knew about Senthil's mental condition. Ramachandran repeated what he had told us earlier in the evening. He was surprised to hear about Senthil's incarceration in the asylum.

On the occasion when he had taken Senthil home, he had met his father and urged him to take the boy to a doctor. The man had answered that he had no belief in doctors and hospitals and he was treating Senthil very effectively at home.

'The boy told me nothing about his hospitalization, except to echo his father's opinion,' Ramachandran frowned.

'Is this the man you met?'

Lalli showed him the dead man's face on the iPad.

Ramachandran exclaimed in horror, clapping a hand to his brow. The very next instant he narrowed his eyes, took off his spectacles and polished them, set them back with great deliberation and steeled himself to take another look.

'This is not the man I met,' he said. 'Yes, I'm quite certain this is not Senthil's father.'

'Perhaps you're mistaken about the identity of the man you met earlier?' Lalli suggested.

'No. That was his father—or rather, that was the man known as Subbu Bhagavathar. He was not alone when we got there. There was a friend with him, discussing the date for a Harikatha. He addressed him as Bhagavathar, and mentioned to me that Subbu Bhagavathar's Harikatha was an annual event in his temple. The man I met was definitely Senthil's father. This is not the same man, though there's a definite resemblance. Subbu Bhagavathar has a large scar on his forehead. What an irony, this face is without blemish.'

'How many times have you met Senthil?'

'That's easily answered, he comes on the first Friday of every month, at around eleven in the morning. So counting from Ganesh Chathurthi last year—'

'Apart from these visits?'

'Never.'

'Has he ever sung on these visits, apart from the first occasion you mentioned?'

'Oh, several times. He sings Thevaram. Amazing memory, perfect diction, and an instinctivc understanding of the emotion. I had every intention of learning from him, but I didn't want to burden the boy with a request.'

'He understood the philosophy of the poetry, do you think? It's very complex.'

'Yes, he did. On one occasion, he picked up a small sandalwood carving of a violently charging elephant from my desk and recited:

Marrathhai maraitthadu mamadayaanai
Marrathil maraindadu mamadayaanai
Paratthai maraitthadu paamudal putham
Parrathil marainthadu paamudal puthame.[3]

That is Tirumoolar's poetry, the most complex of all.'

'You said he had an amazing memory. Why?'

'One day I was singing a song he had never heard before, he exclaimed over the beauty of the lyrics. When I stopped, he recited the poem at once, flawlessly.'

---

3. The intoxicated elephant hid the wood
The intoxicated elephant hid in the wood.
(Even so) The Truth hides the elements
The Truth is hidden in the elements.

'Have you ever witnessed him angry or upset?'

'Upset, certainly. I mentioned the instance earlier this evening. He begged me not to sing *Kadambari priyai*. I sang, defying him, and he had a seizure. Afterwards, on the way home, he wept and reproached me bitterly for bringing on the fit.'

'How did you answer him?'

Ramachandran made a helpless gesture. 'What could I say but beg his forgiveness?'

'You apologized?'

'Apology cannot suffice. I had injured him knowingly.'

'Was he angry? Did he sulk?'

'He was in too much pain to sulk. Oh, I remember now—he did ask me not to mention before his father what had brought on the fit. It would make his father very angry, he said. Angry with me? I asked. He shook his head and said the song would anger his father. He didn't explain, and I didn't ask.'

It sounded like more of Senthil's ravings to me.

'Has he ever seemed heroic or transformed when he declaimed poetry?'

'Heroic, yes, if that was the emotion of the poem. If by transformed you mean ecstatic or transcendent—no. But at the same time, the poetry was very real to him. I'd go so far to say it was his inner reality. He existed within it.'

'Have you ever noticed a violent gesture or expression?'

'Never. He said people teased him often because

he was different. They made fun of him. It used to hurt him when he was younger, but it didn't hurt him anymore. They tried to get him angry, but he found that difficult. I asked why. He smiled and said "*Anbe Sivam*".[4] I realized he wasn't repeating a maxim. It was simply the easiest choice for him. To show love was to be at peace.'

Ramachandran shut his eyes to refuse either the saintly memory of this boy or his present satanic avatar. Or perhaps he wished to reject them both.

Lalli asked, 'Will you see him?'

'Is he here?'

'In the cell.'

'Where is his father?'

'We don't know yet.'

'Perhaps he should see his father before he sees me.'

'He's asked for you.'

'He's also accused me of abetting the murder.'

'That was before. He has no memory of that now.'

'I don't understand.'

Lalli gave him the gist of her interview with Senthil.

Shukla, who had been silent so far, said, 'He was found holding the murder weapon, covered with blood. He denies everything. He claims he has no memory.'

---

4. Love alone is Divinity, the core belief of Tamil Saivism.

'But you think he might be lying.'

Shukla nodded.

'You think I might be lying too.'

'It is possible.'

'What do you want me to do?' Ramachandran asked Lalli helplessly.

'Just talk with Senthil.'

'Alone?'

'If you can bear it.'

'No. I don't think I can. I don't know what to say to him. I can't meet his eye. This is not the boy I know.'

'I want to see if you are the man he knows.'

Ramachandran was led away to the rat chamber. We settled down in the cat chamber to watch the meeting between him and Senthil.

The cat joined us, jumping into the chair Ramachandran had vacated. We watched Senthil being escorted in by the constables.

When he caught sight of Ramachandran, Senthil uttered a cry of relief. 'You've come, Mama! I knew you would. I told them you would.'

Ramachandran nodded, but made no reply.

'Have they told you what's happened?' Senthil asked. 'I can make no sense of it. Can you?'

'No.'

'My chittappa has been murdered. And they say I murdered him. Is that possible?'

Ramachandran was silent.

'Why are you quiet? You cannot believe I am a murderer, surely? Oh, tell me you think I cannot have done it. If you think as they do, who is left? Who will believe me?'

'I believe you.' The words were torn out of Ramachandran.

Senthil said after a long silence, 'You're just saying that to shut me up. I didn't think you'd do that.'

'I'm not. I believe in your innocence.'

'They didn't show you the photos, then.'

'They did.'

'Not the one of me covered in blood.'

'No. Not that one.'

'Ask to see that. Then come back and tell me if you still believe me.' He rose with a sort of ragged pride and made for the door.

'Senthil. Wait, son. Tell me what happened.'

'Afterwards.'

Ramachandran looked around helplessly and waited for rescue.

Lalli showed him all the pictures. Ramachandran sat through it in a clench of revulsion. 'I want to see him now,' he said suddenly. 'Please. I must see him now.'

Once more we watched Senthil enter, but this time, he seemed to have the faintest swagger. He flinched when one of the constables touched him. When they turned to leave, he asked them to stay.

He did not sit down, but looked a question at Ramachandran.

'I've seen the picture. Your picture. I've seen all the pictures,' Ramachandran said.

'And now?'

'I cannot believe you have it in you to commit such a crime,' Ramachandran spoke with slow distinctness. 'It is not because I have any faith in you that I say this. I don't know you well enough for that. But I know you lack the cruelty to do this. Therefore, I believe you are innocent of this crime.'

'You can see me there covered with blood.'

'Yes. Sometimes things are not what they seem.'

'Then what do you advise me to do?'

'Trust in yourself. Wait. First, your father must be found.'

'My father will not believe me innocent.'

'Why not?'

'He says I'm not responsible for my actions when I have a fit.'

'I see. Do you believe you killed this man, Senthil?'

'No. I did not kill him.'

'Then two people believe in your innocence now. That's all I can say at this moment.'

'I thank you.' And folding his hands in gratitude, Senthil left the room.

Shaktivel had been sent in pursuit of the missing father. Shukla was quite confident Shaktivel would find him, and I wondered why Lalli endorsed that.

As Ramachandran left, he asked Lalli, 'Did you find what you were looking for?'

'No.'

'You will.'

I wondered at that, too.

A little past midnight, Shaktivel phoned to say Subbu Bhagavathar had been found. He was in Sion Hospital with a head injury. He had been brought in unconscious an hour ago. He was awake now, but Shaktivel hadn't questioned him as yet. Subbu had been riding pillion with a friend when a passing car hit them. The highway police had brought them in, the friend was DOA.

'Let's go home, Sita,' Lalli murmured wearily.

There was no conversation on the way home. Lalli's exhaustion was palpable. It was all I could do to persuade her to sip some hot milk and rest. Something had changed in her. In a strange way, the turbulent day had brought relief.

I was awake when I heard Savio's bike at the gate. It was a little past five.

It had been an all-nighter, evidently—he had joined Shukla at Sion. His eyes met mine with anxiety.

'She's asleep,' I assured him.

'Something's happened, hasn't it?'

'Yes, this murder's brought her some relief,' I blurted.

I got him his usual comfort food—a cup of hot chocolate and two coconut biscuits, and started the coffee. We faced each other across the table. This was question hour.

'Why am I being kept out of this, Sita?' he demanded angrily. 'Even Shukla knows.'

'What?'

'Whatever it is I don't.'

'I'll tell you what Shukla knows. Lalli told him she's trying to solve a problem, and she might need his help.'

'Why his and not mine?' He sounded sixteen.

'Because of the nature of the problem.'

'Which I suppose you know.'

'Yes.'

'And won't tell me.'

'No. And not just because Lalli wants it so. Because you'll take it on yourself, all of it.'

'So what?'

'Never mind, Savio, we'll all know soon enough what it is. That's when—'

'It hits the fan?'

'Right.'

He leaned his head against me, as a child would. It was almost more than I could bear.

Shukla and Shaktivel arrived, interrupting our peaceful hour in the kitchen. Savio took them off my hands.

I heard Lalli singing in the bathroom. It was the song that had brought on Senthil's seizure in Ramachandran's place, *Kadambari priyai*.

Lalli's voice held a wistful note. It reminded me of a rainy morning when I had walked past a kadamba tree. I hadn't noticed it till the wet green scent of rain was jolted by a spicy drift. Sensuous but canny, it was the breath of the golden globes of florets high up on the tree. It infected me with uncertainty and desire. There was something dangerous too, about the perfume, a menace of pain, afterwards.

I returned to the comforting task at hand.

Savio had peeled the shallots already. They glistened in a white ceramic bowl. Amethyst teardrops, pretending innocence, more lavender than onion.

I was in no mood for such hypocrisy. I slashed the skillet with ghee, scattered mustard, raised the heat till the grains protested, and then tossed in those dissembling juveniles. There—that should larn them.

They weren't bruised enough to make me weep, so they kept their milky breath as they hit the skillet. The first sear, as they sweated out moisture, was more armpit than aroma. Rough, adolescent, ammoniacal, crass. But, in the next few minutes, they were getting there. They lost opalescence, turning glassy as invisible cell walls cracked up, leaking out a chemical gush of sugars and sulfides.

A minute more and they would brown to a restaurant gunk.

I flung a handful of curry leaves at them, added the merest pinch of turmeric, a few grains of sugar. Sprinkling just enough water to raise an outraged hiss, I slammed on the lid and stepped back. If that didn't educate the truth out of them, nothing could.

Shukla wandered in just as I lifted the lid. I had misjudged those babies. There was nothing crass about the cloud of steam that welled out. It had lost its slapstick guffaw and turned witty. When I added the ground masala, those shallots would skip about, nimble with repartee.

'You are not using powder for sambar,' Shukla observed disapprovingly. 'Mrs Shukla has very good powder. Very quick. Two spoons. I am myself able to make. Now khiru from the shop plus powder and idli sambar within minutes for Sunday breakfast.'

'She'll make a cook of you yet, Shukla.'

'What is happening to Lalli, Sita? Are you sure no serious illness?'

'Everybody seems to be sure, Shukla.'

'But you're scared.'

I sank into a chair, suddenly tired.

'She told me just now to ask you to explain.'

This was going to be difficult. I was not prepared to tell Shukla that Lalli thought she had committed a murder and was trying to summon up its details.

Finally, I told him no more than I had told Savio. 'She's trying to remember something, and she can't.'

'Personal?'

'Yes.'

'Bad personal.'

'Yes.'

'So how far she's got?'

I shook my head. 'She can only remember some music, but even that she's unsure about.'

'So Ramchandar is singing with wife to provide clues.'

'Right.'

'But instead he becomes mixed up in murder. Come on, let's go, Sita. Just now Shaktivel has questioned Senthil's father.'

'You rely on him a lot.'

'Bright boy. Brilliant.'

'But no brain.'

We exchanged a high five and joined the others.

'So, Shaktivel, tell us how you found Senthil's father last night,' Lalli said.

Shaktivel had smartened up considerably this morning. His hair had the lacquered gloss of some vicious pomade, and his chubby cheeks had been patted with aftershave.

'Two possibilities are there, madam—'

'Shaktivel, please call me Lalli, everybody does.'

'I am knowing that, madam, but I am not able at present moment.'

'Very well, continue.'

'Only two possibilities—father is either guilty or

innocent. If innocent he will return home at usual time. But he did not. Therefore, choosing path of innocence, I pursued enquiries. No answer on his mobile, still.'

'And what did you find?'

'Nothing. Place of enquiry, temple, but they were not knowing anything there. Where does he usually go? I asked. Here and there for Harikatha, they said. Useless. Before this I had asked Senthil when he was expecting his father home, and he said by six o'clock. So Harikatha explanation cancelled, as not possible father goes without son's knowledge, as they are performing together. So, some small errand. But then, keeping to path of innocence, still, why he has not returned home? Senthil has no mobile, but father has, and we can trace calls. I was going to do that next, but continuing on path of innocence I thought such a man will not return home only if he is injured or dead. So I checked road accidents first. Highway police said they had a man who fits the description. I went there and gave him missed call, mobile rang in his pocket. Missing person found.'

'Still on path of innocence?'

'Hundred per cent, madam. If guilty he would not be found.'

'Why not? He could still have been hit by a car.'

'But would he be riding pillion with a friend?'

'The friend may have conspired with him to murder his brother.'

'No, madam. Very respectable man, this friend. Temple trustee. He had gone to Nerul temple. He was having lunch there at the time of murder. Subbu Bhagavathar reached there at three p.m. They left together at five-thirty p.m. These details I am just now receiving from Kalgutkar.'

'That still does not keep him on the path of innocence, as you put it,' Lalli frowned.

'Only hippopotamously, madam. I am aware of bogus innocence.' He turned to Shukla. 'Sir, madam is not knowing of our campaign, I think.'

'Later, Shaktivel. Now continue.' Shukla was in an agony of embarrassment, making me mighty curious about this campaign. Savio, glowering at the company, seemed to have switched off altogether.

'So did you question this Subbu Bhagavathar?' Lalli asked.

'Five a.m. Till then he was sleeping, snoring very hard. Doctors refused to wake him up saying sleep may not be normal. So I asked why can't you tell if sleep is normal or dangerous? What is the use of being doctor if you can't tell? So immediately they decided now patient cannot be questioned for next twenty-four hours. But I said this is homicide. I am not moving from bedside. Moment he wakes up, I will question.' He paused, expecting applause.

'What happened at five a.m.?'

'I have video.'

Out came Shukla's trusty iPad.

'Because of head injury, I am thinking mother tongue is better, so I am questioning him in Tamil, but stubbornly every time he is answering in Hindi-Marathi.'

I didn't blame the guy. Shaktivel's Tamil was enough to give anyone a head injury.

Subbu Bhagavathar's surly appearance, so very different from the dead man's mask of calm, made it difficult to concede the resemblance. But they were, in fact, very alike. Adding to the resemblance now was the fact that Subbu Bhagavathar's shoulder-length hair hung loose instead of being bundled in the knot usual with men of his occupation.

Shaktivel opened the interview with standard questions about name, address, occupation. When it came to family, Shaktivel pushed on beyond.

'How many brothers and sisters do you have?'

'How does that matter?' Subbu retaliated with energy. 'What does that have to do with my accident?'

This is when Shaktivel got ominous. 'I am not interviewing you about your accident.'

'No? Then what is this about? Can't it wait? My head is splitting.'

'It's likely to shatter by the time I finish. How many brothers and sisters do you have?'

'One brother, Narayanan.'

'Address?'

'He comes and goes, useless fellow sleeps in the temple, can't hold on to a job.'

'Younger or older to you?'

'Younger, by two years.'

'When did you last see him?'

'Yesterday—no, the day before, if today is tomorrow. What time is it?'

'Five a.m.'

'Five a.m. Tuesday?'

'Yes.'

'Then I saw Narayanan on Sunday evening. He had dinner with us, then he left around nine o'clock.'

'Where did he go?'

'I didn't ask. I never ask, dreading the answer.'

'Drink?'

'No, he doesn't drink. Gambles. Bets on anything. Whatever he wins, he spends on women.'

'What did you do Monday morning?'

'Let me see,' Subbu frowned, kneading his temples. 'Monday. Senthil—my son—set off as usual around ten. He has his route mapped out. Every day a different place. Mondays he's right here in Sion. I expected him to take his lunch in the temple, so I set out at about ten-fifteen. I had to go to Nerul a little later. I checked with the temple to see if they had anything for me. After that I set out, may have been around noon. Waited very long for a bus, and then the bus had a breakdown past the check naka, so I waited there again. It was three p.m. when I reached Nerul, absolutely famished. I finished my business there in the temple. I met my good friend Tyagu, he said if I hung around a bit he would give me a lift home. I remember I got on his scooter, remember a big red hoarding flashing past, I was trying to read it and then—bam! Can't remember anything after that. The doctor said a car hit us. What about Tyagu? Is he all right?'

'Your friend Tyagarajan was killed on the spot.'

Subbu Bhagavathar struck his forehead in despair. 'And I am alive, miserable sinner that I am. His poor wife—do they know already? I must go there, immediately.' He scrambled out of bed.

Shaktivel thrust him back on the pillows.

'Is this your brother?' Without preamble, Shaktivel confronted him with the picture of the murdered man.

Shrinking back in horror, Subbu Bhagavathar gave a wordless howl of protest.

'Your brother was murdered in your house this afternoon.'

Shaktivel then showed him the picture of Senthil drenched with blood.

Subbu Bhagavathar's response was unexpected.

His long sigh sounded very like relief. 'So he's done it finally,' he said. 'I always knew this day would come. Sir, my son has a mental illness. He is not responsible for his actions. He has done this terrible deed, but he has these seizures, fits, and spells of confusion follow. He was in Thana asylum for six months last year. Poor boy! What a heinous sin he has committed! What can save him now?'

After some more incoherent exclamations and appeals to every god and goddess in the pantheon Subbu Bhagavathar finally asked, 'Have you arrested my son?'

'He's in the lock up.'

'Please be kind to him. He is a good boy even though he's a murderer. I brought him up strict, very religious, and now all that is just a waste. When can I see him?'

'We'll let you know.'

Shaktivel's selfie signed off.

'Father is telling the truth,' Shukla declared. 'Boy is mental case. He has murdered no-good uncle in fit of temporary insanity. Good lawyer will get him committed. End of story.'

But it wasn't.

We were just sitting down to lunch when Ramachandran rang the doorbell. With him was Senthil.

Surprise deepened as we took in the young man standing next to Ramachandran. This was not the Senthil we knew.

'Twin,' Ramachandran stated by way of explanation.

The young man came forward. 'I'm the one who ran away.'

'Senthil never mentioned a brother, leave alone a twin,' Ramachandran said.

'He may not remember me. I don't remember him. But I do know he exists.'

'What is your name?' Lalli asked.

'Guru.'

They might be twins, but the two young men were exact opposites. Guru was keen as a knife. His whiplash gaze took us in coolly. He was in herd couture, jeans and a tee. He addressed us in English, and seemed educated.

'Why are we talking at the doorstep, come in please. Ramachandran, you too,' Lalli invited. 'So Guru, you're a musician too, I see. Violin?'

Guru was as taken aback as I was.

'Why—yes. How do you know?'

'It's my job. You've been playing since you were what—ten? Twelve?'

'Twelve. I'm not a professional or anything of that sort. I just play.'

'But very seriously.'

He laughed. 'I enjoy it.'

It was amazing what that laugh did to his face. Now he was just a carefree kid, the torment lifted clean off him.

That was it—that was what made the two bothers so similar. Their features were not identical, but they had been engraved into the same mask of torment over years.

That was puzzling. Their lives had been separate for most of their young lives, and yet their torment had been the same.

'But I see we've interrupted your lunch. Please don't let the food get cold. I can wait.'

'But you must join us!'

'Thank you, but Uncle made me eat with him.' He acknowledged Ramachandran with an expressive glance. 'He practically forced me, or I could not have swallowed a morsel until I found out the truth.' That said, his face resumed its hauteur. He seemed to retreat into some invisible zone. As he took a seat against the wall, he practically effaced himself.

Ramachandran rose. 'Ponni has a programme this evening. Yesterday's business has upset her, and I must help her pick the songs. I'll be back if you want me.'

'Please return, I do need you here,' Lalli said. 'In half an hour?'

We hurried through lunch in ten minutes. I stole a glance at Guru as I cleared up. He met my look with one so challenging, I hurried away.

Savio joined me. We worked swiftly, and as usual the wordless rhythm restored us.

It was hot in the kitchen.

Savio gathered up my hair and knotted it into a chignon. My neck felt deliciously cool. I leaned against his solidity and shut my eyes, wondering why life could not always be like this moment.

Lalli was talking music animatedly with Guru. Or, rather, she was drawing him out, and his words had enlivened her. Shukla and Shaktivel were in a huddle. Shukla muttered in an undertone, 'Shaktivel has not heard any rumour of runaway brother. This is complete four-twenty, so why is Lalli giving him so much bhaav?'

'Why should he turn up just now?' I countered. 'All of a sudden, just after the murder, he remembers his old family? It's too pat.'

'Unless, of course, the murder occurred because he remembered his old family,' Savio pointed out.

That was an angle I hadn't considered.

Lalli was treating this Guru like just another kid who had dropped in for a chat.

'I don't get the violin bit,' I murmured to Savio.

'Me also,' Shukla added.

'He's right-handed, but his left is more muscular, finger pads are calloused. Notice how he's always protecting his left hand?' Savio explained.

Ramachandran returned, looking even more disgruntled.

'Ah, there you are, Ramachandran, I was waiting for you,' Lalli greeted him. 'Guru has just been telling me how he started learning the violin. I hope we can hear him play some time.'

'Be glad to. Do you have any favourites?'

'A capriccio perhaps? Paganini?'

Guru laughed out aloud. 'You're a dangerous lady.'

'It's dangerous music. I heard Madoyan play all twenty-four capricci without interruption and entirely from memory—'

'Nikolay Madoyan? You're kidding, right?'

'No. 4th November 2003. San Donato Church, in Genoa. It was an unexpected bonus! I was up in the bell tower, hiding. Listening to those notes floating up was like being transported to a different galaxy. But your story intrigues me, Guru. Do you remember what that first tune was? The one you picked out on Raymond's violin?' She turned to us to explain. 'Guru was working as a canteen boy in a college, he told me. One afternoon—we won't ask how—he found himself alone with the music teacher's violin. He kept it a secret for a week, while the music teacher of course went crazy looking for it. When he had cracked the mystery and managed to get a tune out of it, he returned it to Raymond Gomes. The only way he could convince Raymond he hadn't meant to steal it was to play a tune. And that's the one I want to hear!'

'I'm afraid I can't sing it for you,' Guru said. 'My throat has a permanent frog in it. I'll bring my instrument whenever you want.'

'Keyboard?' Ramachandran ventured. 'I have a small one.'

'You're a musician, Uncle?'

'No, my wife is. I'll be back.'

'I am going now, madam,' Shaktivel rose, adjusting his belt that seemed alarmingly tight. 'Murder has to be solved, no time for musical performance.'

'Please go ahead and solve your murder, Shaktivel,

while we enjoy the music,' Lalli said graciously, with no hint of sarcasm. I was surprised at the change in her. Her eyes laughed, her face was eager and flushed. She was so tense she seemed to quiver.

'Sit down, Shaktivel!' Shukla ordered.

'No, Shukla, the boy is right, let him go. He is of no use here. Be sure to let us know when you've solved the case.' Lalli held the door open for him.

Ramachandran returned with a small synthesizer, and after a few minutes spent in getting acquainted, Guru hit the keyboard.

Not especially curious, I prepared my usual polite response.

But if I hadn't noticed Lalli's warning look at Ramachandran, I too might have cried out after the first few notes. This was neither Paganini's capriccio nor any of Raymond Gomes' 'exercises'. Played with more verve than five-year-old Vasu ever gave it, the tune that bounced off the keyboard was the only Dikshitar *kriti* I knew, *Shyamale meenakshi*.

'What a pretty tune,' Lalli exclaimed with magnificent guile. 'Did you make it up?'

'No, I sort of remembered it, I guess.'

'So how old were you when you ran away from home?'

'Seven.'

'And do you know why?'

'No. I can't remember that. But nothing will make me ever go back, nothing can.'

'And yet you did, didn't you?'

'Yes. Because I ran into my uncle.'

'You recognized him?'

'No, he recognized me. I was walking to work when someone called out, "Guru!" I can't explain it, but the voice made my heart stop. I felt faint. I stopped dead in my tracks. And then when he came up to me, I knew he was my chittappa. I mean—I can't understand how, I don't remember my parents or my brother or anything at all of my old life. But I knew him at once. And he said, "Guru, is it really you, after all these years?" How did he recognize me? Now of course I know it was because my twin resembles me, but that day, it was last Tuesday, I didn't even remember I had a twin.'

'So how did that encounter affect you?'

'I could do nothing at work all day. I work at a computer company. We make electronic stuff. I met him after work at a café—I got the feeling he would be glad of a meal. It wasn't easy talking to him. I've forgotten the language, the people, their ways. It was terrible to learn my mother was dead. I couldn't remember her face. That was—that is awful. I don't particularly want to go back. I've made a life for myself, I don't even know if I want that old life. They've lived without me so long. But Chittappa told me about Senthil. I had forgotten him. I wanted to meet him. I wasn't keen on meeting my dad. Maybe I felt guilty for having run away. Maybe I'm angry he didn't even look for me. Why would he want to see me now?'

'But you met your chittappa again.'

'Yes. I—I like him. It just felt easy talking to him.'

'Just now you said it was difficult,' Shukla growled.

'Did I? Yes, it was, the first time. Then I started looking forward to meeting him. I met him again on Sunday night. He phoned me around nine and I met him at the same place—'

'Which is?'

'This small café, Light of Madras. I used to work there before I got the college canteen job. They were good to me, so I've kept in touch.'

'So it was the first place that took you in after you'd run away?'

'Yeah. For a year it was mostly station platforms, under bridges, that sort of thing. I kept running. I only knew I had to run as far as I could. Looking back, I can't imagine what it must have been like. Don't remember most of it.'

'What happened on Sunday night between you and your Chittappa?'

'He told me he was going to arrange for a family reunion. I agreed to leave it to him. He gave me an address and asked me to come there on Tuesday morning—that's today—at eleven. So I asked for the day off, and went there after spending a sleepless night worried sick. But nothing could have warned me the homecoming would be like this!'

'What happened when you got there?'

'What happened? Everything happened. A woman caught sight of me and screamed. A crowd collected. At first a few people shouted, "Murderer!" But soon they were all silent, just staring at me, realizing in a few minutes, that I was not Senthil. By then a havaldar came up and asked me who I was. The next thing I know, I was hauled to the chowki. They took my statement. Then they told me Senthil had murdered Chittappa. I couldn't believe it. They said Senthil was insane. I couldn't believe that either. I wanted to meet someone who could help me—so they showed me the address Senthil had given them, Ramachandran Uncle's. I decided if Senthil trusted him, I would too. So I came here.'

Ramachandran essayed to speak, then lapsed into silence.

Lalli urged him to speak his thought.

'It's irrelevant, really. I was about to ask what other tunes came naturally to you.'

'Strange you should ask. Ever since I met Chittappa, I've been playing new tunes, I suppose they're all from my childhood, but the strangest thing is they come and go at will. I can't recall them when I want to.'

With a glance at Lalli, Ramachandran hummed *Shyamale meenakshi* under his breath, then sang the simple *swaram*. He was halfway through when Guru's voice joined his. His eyes were closed, his face tranquil, with a frightening resemblance to the mask of the dead man.

As Ramachandran took up the lyrics of the song, Guru accompanied him flawlessly. When he opened his eyes, he looked trapped. He rose hastily.

'I—I don't want to do this. I can't. I'm sorry. I want to help Senthil, but I can't. I don't want to meet him, or my dad. I want nothing to do with them. Nothing!' His voice rose. He was panting in agitation. He looked as if he might bite. And all the while I noticed his left hand was held in against his chest, bunching up his tee.

'You need time to face this, Guru,' Lalli said gently. 'It's true we need your help. Senthil needs your help. But it's up to you. We have your address at the chowki. Don't disappear.'

'Fat chance of that, with cops after me.'

'You know my house now,' Ramachandran said. 'If you ever need a roof, come here.'

'Really?' Guru was taken aback.

'Really.'

'Why?'

'I would like to hear Paganini too.'

Guru broke down, kneading his temples very like Senthil had.

Savio got up, but Lalli stalled him with a gesture. We let Guru get over the worst. I got him a mug of chocolate and Savio's coconut biscuits.

'Maybe he's the murderer,' Shukla muttered helpfully as I passed him.

I spilled the cocoa, the biscuits slid to the floor. Shukla jumped up contritely, crushing them underfoot.

In the confusion that followed, my irritation at Shukla's embarrassment kept me from noticing that Guru had left, accompanied by Savio.

Ramachandran was about to leave when Shukla stopped him.

'Ramchandarji, you can co-operate with police.'

'What do you mean, Inspector? Another interrogation?' He looked at Lalli, although he addressed Shukla.

'I think you've answered all Savio's questions,' Lalli said. 'Shukla has something else in mind.'

'I am considering applying same music test to Senthil. It may bring out the truth.'

'No.'

Shukla was taken aback.

'I won't torment Senthil even if I have to go to jail for it,' Ramachandran retorted angrily. 'I'm sorry I put this boy through such anguish. I had no business doing that. I will not be party to any such test, Inspector Shukla. Now I would like to go home.'

Shukla began protesting, but Lalli silenced him. 'I agree with you, Ramachandran. You have no further part to play in this case. If you wish to help Senthil, you're a free agent. It goes without saying, that if

Senthil perceives you as part of the police, he won't speak with you. For my part, I would be grateful if you kept in touch with the boy.'

Ramachandran's face relaxed. 'I sincerely believe in Senthil's innocence. I would like to talk with his father. Will that be possible?'

'Certainly, once the police have finished questioning him.'

'Thank you, Lalli. I'll be in touch, Sita.' And picking up his keyboard, Ramachandran left.

'Ramchandarji is not bothered about murder,' Shukla stated. 'There is blackness in the dal here also. Why for he is so good to these boys? One is murderer, the other is pakka mavali, must be charge-sheeter, I'm sure.'

'Guru? Why do you say that, Shukla?' Lalli asked.

'Look at his face, so tight, so able to laugh. Talking about gaana bajana when just now he has found own uncle murdered, full family in trouble. And how after so many years he meets this uncle and turns up just like that? Too much coincidence for Shukla.'

'Too much blackness in dal again?' I asked.

'Arre, Sita, in this case dal is complete black. Totally, as teenagers are saying for everything. Toaddlly, like that.'

'So what's your theory, Shukla?' Lalli asked.

'Double conspiracy. Both brothers. Guru is the brain. Senthil does what Guru says. Who struck the blow? Definitely Guru. Then he runs away, leaving Senthil to take the blame.'

'And you think Guru is confident Senthil won't rat on him?' I asked.

'Rats and cats I am not knowing, Sita. But this Guru is pakka dhobhi ka kutta. He has done this to get something, so Shukla asks *cui bono*? You know that, Sita? It is Latin. Ancient European language spoken by very modern Indian. What it means? Who gains? Who profits from this murder? What did this uncle have which the boys wanted? Money? Gold? Jewellery?'

'Do you really think the uncle hid wealth, Shukla? By all accounts he didn't know where his next meal was coming from,' Lalli protested.

'Anything is possible—from lottery ticket to family hairs on loom. What is your idea, Lalli?'

'I have none at present. I'd like to speak with the father once he's out of hospital. Meanwhile, Shukla, what do the neighbours say about this uncle?'

'Nobody seems to know him. But yes, they've seen him, but didn't think they were brothers. Hairstyle and dress too different. Brother is mostly pant shirt, other one is dhoti. Plus brother's hair is Amitabh Bachchan, and mahant is making jooda behind baldness. It is too much for public to digest.'

He paused thoughtfully. 'Shukla is waiting for instructions in personal matter, Lalli.'

'I know. Let it be for now, Shukla. Once this case is solved, we'll see.'

'Savio has gone there so that I can be free for you. Any moment. Day or night. Sita is dentating with me already.'

And leaving us to contemplate this horrid picture, Shukla made his exit.

It was not yet six, but the clouds had advanced twilight. The room was laved in its lilac glow. I brought Lalli a cup of tea, made the way she liked it; very light, with a single leaf of bruised mint, and a squeeze of lemon.

Neither of us had eaten much lunch. I made some toast and carried the hot buttered triangles out to the balcony along with a small pot of marmalade I had been hoarding as a surprise.

Unlike Lalli's hearty orange, this marmalade was a dodgy lime green.

Lalli inhaled, then fished out a curl of zest with the knife tip.

I held my breath.

She dug in the knife and slathered her toast. 'Delicious!'

I had broken all the rules and struck out on this one.

Citrus limetta, our mosambi or chattukkudi, is a much abused fruit. It is battered on sight. The rind's avulsed and flung aside, the fruit quartered and mangled and its lifeblood swilled greedily, gulped for its benefits, never savoured for its delights.

Those delights begin with the smooth tight-pored skin, unyielding under the persuasive fingernail. No mist of irritating oil sprays your eye: no orange, this. You can excoriate the cuticle, leaving a bright green trail, but that's as far as you'll get. You could, of course, bruise your own cuticles and morcellate the peel. The mosambi will then turn its back on you and wall itself within a thick wadding of pith. Far more intelligent, then, to reach for the knife, if only to release the principal delight of this fruit—its fragrance.

A neat incision leaves a trace of yellow-green oil on the knife's edge. A minute later, you can smell the tender scent, vibrating clear as a bell in the still air. It doesn't knock you flat like the robust scent of a Nagpur mandarin.

The Nagpur mandarin is the Muhammad Ali of citrus scents: it flits like a butterfly, stings like a bee. The mosambi is a pacifist. It doesn't urge you to muscle up and spar.

Orange compels the crossword. Mosambi makes you look up from your book. Orange has the texture of kanjivaram silk, a slide of luxury against the skin. Mosambi is muslin, it entraps you in its mesh of light.

But the scent of mosambi is a surface pleasure, a top note quickly volatilized at body temperature, leaving a vague gumminess as dry down. It hints of vapidity.

There are other challenges. Unwrap each segment, and you've lost already much of the fruit's felicity.

There are fruits in which the arils stand apart from their cellophane wrappers, but these are chancy.

Most mosambis have their juice tightly packaged in clingfilm, tear it off at your peril.

The best way to get the most out of your mosambi is to chomp the segment whole. The usually intense sweetness is tamped down by the mild bitterness of the fibre. It's a fruit with no sense of humour.

Would it retain its character in a jam?

The lack of tartness is easily remedied, but bitterness has a way of dulling the senses, unforgivable in a marmalade.

Still, I had taken the plunge and was pleasantly surprised.

I had expected the scent to turn into the febrile odour of boiled fibre, but the zest had kept its fragrance.

It had kept its bitterness too, but it was the bicker of small grievances.

It takes a citron to bleed the grand tincture of tragedy.

This was girlie marmalade, and I recognized the tune that went with it. It was the song Lalli had been singing in her bath, *Kadambari priyai*....

'You should have let Shukla persuade Ramachandran,' I blurted out, surprising the thought.

'Really? I want Ramachandran free of all this.

He's not a man who should be dragged into this mess.'

'Because you want him to get the truth out of Senthil.'

'Oh no! Because I want him to get the truth out of *me*.'

The look of fear had returned to her eyes. This case had not distracted her for a moment from her quest.

'I'm close, so close, Sita. At the edge of seeing it—but I can't.'

'What did that last song of Ramachandran's remind you of?' I couldn't for the life of me recall either the words or the melody. It was an unfamiliar *raagam* too.

'Aha. I see you're applying the Ramachandran Trick.'

I laughed. 'Like this marmalade makes me understand *Kadambari priyai*.'

'How?'

'Pure girlitude. Dikshitar saw a girl all dressed up and bejewelled, a little dazed by her first glimpse in a mirror, a little smug at her heady sexiness—and he's moved by that delicate balance of danger and innocence. But he knows it's fleeting—like this marmalade. So a *raagam* of tremulous beauty, where the moment is everything.'

'Then I'll tell you what I heard in that last song—I heard another song, Sita, and I couldn't identify it.'

'What do you mean?'

'I heard someone *singing another song*. As if Ramachandran's song were remembering this one. I heard the memory of his song.'

It sounded impossible.

'I know. I'm almost ashamed to tell you. There's no logic to it,' she sighed. 'But then, I didn't expect there would be.'

'What next?'

She shook her head and retreated into silence.

Having left Lalli pensive last night, I expected to find her sleepless, perched on the beige sofa in bright-eyed anxiety. The scent of coffee woke me at half past five. Lalli hadn't been on her usual morning run for more than a month now. I hurried out of bed, worried the sudden exertion might be too much for her.

She was in the kitchen, sifting flour while waiting for the coffee. She looked much more herself than she had been yesterday.

'Did you go for your run?'

'No, I'm not ready for that yet. Just a brisk walk.'

'What are you making?'

She shrugged. It was rice flour.

'Karakarapriya?'

'She eludes me. I thought—But then, Sita, you know, I'm no good at making kai murrukku, so the usual.'

That reminded me of what I had been about to tell her on our way to Sion chowki.

'Lalli, your memory of kai murukku is not from Karakarapriya. It's from Shukla's murukku, the one we brought from Ambarnath.'

'Sita! I had forgotten that.' She slumped into a chair, all her excitement drained. 'One more dead end, then. What am I going to do?' She buried her face in her hands, fingers clawing her hair.

I set our mugs of coffee down and waited.

Then I said, 'Perhaps it's not a dead end, Lalli. Perhaps you forgot it for a reason.'

'Don't go all Freud on me, Sita.'

I was, a bit, I admit. Still the old chauvinist wasn't all wrong.

'What if you think of it as a dream?' I suggested.

'Wish fulfillment?'

'No. What if you keep these memories as they are, disparate, and don't try to rationalize.'

'Ah. You demand a withdrawal of the watchers from my gates of intelligence.'

'That's Freud!'

'No, Schiller. He said it a hundred years before Freud, but hey, everybody gets to it eventually. It's an idea, Sita. Let me see what I can do.'

She put away the flour with some relief.

'You never did tell me what happened at Ambarnath.'

'I'll tell you now,' I said.

Sunday, 13 April
Ambarnath

Shukla turned up that Sunday asking if I'd like a trip to Ambarnath. Sub-Inspector Shaktivel had promised to show him something curious.

'Madrasi festival,' Shaktivel grinned. 'Madam maybe knowing?'

I couldn't think of a festival that coincided with the date.

Ambarnath is a dusty little town. With a thriving Sindhi spillover from Ulhasnagar, it's not really the kind of place you would expect Tamil diaspora.

There was something about Shaktivel that set my teeth on edge. On the drive to Ambarnath, he kept up a mysterious dialogue with Shukla at every intersection.

Shaktivel: *This one is good, sir?*

Shukla: *First class/Useless.*

Shaktivel: *Small or big, sir?*

Shukla: *Big/small.*

So many events have happened since then that I retain a peculiarly selective memory of that day. I remember, for instance, three aged women on the bridge who looked up and muttered as we passed. They didn't actually say *Bubble, bubble, toil and trouble,* but in hindsight they might as well have.

The bridge spanned a nallah that had started life as the river Ulhas, but was now a beast of burden for garbage, a sluggish scavenger that belied its exuberant name. The railings of the bridge, though, were smart with fresh paint.

A moment later, I glimpsed something straight out of a sci-fi film.

A conical monolith.

Definitely extraterrestrial—how else can a mass of stone make such a perfect landing in a dusty town?

The Ambareshwar Temple (tenth century, perhaps eleventh) is one of the few Saivaite shrines in this region that has an uninterrupted history of worship. Most of the others had been pulverized or defaced by Portuguese zealots.

I'd been wanting to see this temple for years.

It was for this, and not for Shaktivel's puzzling 'Madrasi festival' that I'd come along.

Temples have no religious connotation for me, but I'm drawn to them. Like myth, they're museums of human memory.

The temple was very like the Sun Temple in Lonar, which is very like Konark.

I was eager to shake off Shukla and Shaktivel and wander off on my own.

'This side, madam, come this side,' Shaktivel urged.

'I've told you my name, Shaktivel, will you stop calling me madam?'

'Yes, madam,' he assured me.

'Very short-tempered lady,' I heard him remark to Shukla.

Thinking a little balm might be in order, I followed them.

And walked right into a kaleidoscope.

The stone courtyard was an explosion of colour. Out of the temple's monochromatic grey had tumbled gods and goddesses, heroes and apsaras, gandharva and yaksha, exulting in liberation. They spun in vibrant patterns, shadowed or gleaming, tremulous, static, fluid as water, still as stone.

Slowly, the courtyard came into sharp focus.

Yellow.

Intense, joyous, luminous yellow. Yellow flared up everywhere against dark skin.

In perfect complement, viridian and blue shimmered and lost themselves in the prismatic scatter.

I blinked.

Was this a pre-arranged palette?

Yellow followed the eye everywhere. Men, women, children, all wearing yellow. Small gopurams of marigold were being built into miniature chariots.

Yellow-swathed kavadis of bamboo, waiting to be lifted.

'*Arohara!*'

'*Saranam saranam, saravanabhava om!*'

'*Saranam saranam shanmuga saranam!*'

'*Arumuga!*'

'*Arohara!*'

'*Vel! Vel! Vetrivel!*'

The cries, in different degrees of exhortation and encouragement told me this was no ordinary conclave of Murugan worshippers. Couldn't be Thai Pusam, we were already in April.

Of course—Panguni Uthiram, celebrated in Murugan temples with great pomp.

'Sita!'

Shukla's voice interrupted my reverie. He was on the temple steps, waving me over. He had a better vantage, so I joined him, skirting the crowd.

I found Shukla near-mesmerized.

'How it is possible, Sita?' he asked. 'Look at that man, there!'

The object of his wonderment was a man of about fifty, in a yellow veshti, his shaven head smeared with sandalwood paste. He had his back to us, and at first it seemed only his attitude that was strange, legs planted wide, torso tilted back.

I was yet to see what had amazed Shukla.

The man spread out his arms and turned around, very slowly.

I cried out in alarm.

A spear transfixed his face, passing in through one cheek, emerging from the other, its point gleaming gold in the sunshine.

I knew that piercing was symbolic of the

destruction of illusion by Murugan's Vel. With the bearing of the kavadi, it made part of the devotion. I had never seen the event before, and I certainly couldn't have imagined this.

I expected the symbolic vel to be something small and delicate, like an acupuncture needle. Not a hefty three-foot spear that belonged in battle.

The wounds on the devotee's cheek were dusted with vibhuti. I expected a daze of either pain, or some mind-bending chemical, but there was nothing of the sort here. His face was calm and sentient.

This man was as alert as I was.

His eyes met mine gravely, and moved away.

Shukla mopped his forehead. 'How it is possible, Sita?'

'Black magic,' Shaktivel offered.

Shukla looked to me for enlightenment, so I quashed the black magic theory. But I didn't have an alternative to offer.

The celebrants were all dressed in yellow. There were many women among them, most in their sixties. Like the man with the spear, they had been prepared already.

I went down to the courtyard to observe the ritual more closely.

And running up to greet me came Murugan himself.

A boy of ten, as full of mischief as the child in the legend who quizzed the poet Avvaiyar.

This little Murugan was dressed for the role in signature yellow, his forehead glowed with vibhuti, his shaven scalp had a cap of drying sandalwood paste. He wore a garland with great dignity, and raised his vel in greeting with a wide gap-toothed grin, and led me to the group of devotees.

He was the youngest celebrant in a family pierced beyond martyrdom. The father's rippling biceps were pincushions, with dozens of six-inch miniature vels embedded deep.

Grandmother, a little uncomfortable in leaving her shoulders bare above a tightly wound yellow sari, was being prepared by her daughter. Her back and shoulders had been dusted with vibhuti. Her face showed intense concentration, but no pain as her daughter unflinchingly sank steel hooks into her shoulder blades. Each hook dangled a large lemon, its weight plunging the hook deeper in the flesh.

Very soon the ashy expanse of back was beaded with drops of blood, staunched immediately with fresh dabs of vibhuti.

Noticing me flinch, the lady smiled.

'Just a touch of Thiruneer and one feels no pain at all. This is Murugan's grace.'

She wiggled her shoulders to get more comfortable, then stepped forward, perfectly at ease. Next to her a woman my age had just pierced her tongue. She too, like the older lady, showed no pain or anxiety.

'Come on, let's see the Mayil Azhagan!'

The little Murugan took my hand and led me up the steps. 'Look!'

The piercing ritual is *azhagu*, literally beautification.

The word *Muruga* means Beauty, and it is the child-warrior's principal attribute.

I overheard Shukla asking Shaktivel, 'There is a cock on the god's flag, is that why he's called Murga?'

'Must be,' was Shaktivel's sublime answer.

'It's a different language, Shukla,' I said wearily. 'In your neck of the woods you call him Kartik.'

'Kartik is very different. He is having only one head. He is not child but very tiptop hero.'

The child had left us, I caught sight of him in the distance, flitting through a growing cumulus of yellow.

The Mayil Azhagan was just beginning his manifestation.

The young man seated on a plastic stool was still as an effigy. He could have been one of the stone heroes on the wall behind him, so compacted was his stillness.

That lithic intentness commandeered my eye. It was that and only that I noticed. Behind a bar of thick steel, his young face settled into tranquility.

It took a long moment for the truth to sink in. He was not jailed behind that rod. He was transfixed by it. The shining spear had pierced his left cheek and found its way out through the other.

He opened his mouth in a tentative gape.

Steel glinted above his tongue.

With the same experimental slowness, his lips came together again, this time with a slight smile of satisfaction.

All this while, his head was rigid. His eyes moved without the slightest motion of his sturdy, ash-smeared neck.

His head supported a three-tiered gopuram. Swathed in tinsel, it was decorated with pictures of Murugan. The bamboo frame of this construction fitted into his larger, more complicated metal scaffolding.

I found my own slowness of comprehension bewildering. I was taking very long to understand the framework of the azhagu. My eyes saw, but my brain lagged. I now perceived that it was not merely the long steel rod that transfixed him.

A steel scaffolding was bolted on him with a metal belt. Its outer perimeter had two concentric arches of bamboo and steel. This was the *mayil*, the peacock. It fanned over him like a peacock's tail.

The mayil was anchored to his body with a shimmer of steel wires—on looking closer, I discerned them to be fine chains, not wires.

Each chain was connected to his torso by a steel hook sunk deep in the flesh. Two large apples dangled from separate piercings above the nipples. At its free end, each chain ended in a golden vel, completing a fanned out peacock tail. His friends were busy decorating the mayil with jasmine garlands.

That done, a new flurry of activity began.

Two men came forward, and placing two stools on either side of the Azhagan, sat down, feet planted firmly apart, forearms clamped on their thighs, hands grasping their knees.

Almost casually, the Azhagan placed his hands on their shoulders. They rested lightly, but the gesture changed everything.

It was the signal for silence.

The noise retreated and I became aware of a melodious chant. The *kandar shashti kavacham* was being sung by a vibrant tenor. Not only was his voice all steel and honey, but it sculpted in clean lines every word of the poem. Each poetic device sprang out with an air of discovery.

I listened, entranced.

As it drew to an end with a rousing *Sharanam sharanam shanmuga sharanam*, the Mayil Azhagan rose.

His friends on either side took the strain of his mayil on their shoulders as his hands grasped for leverage.

Behind him, several people formed a protective arc.

He was supremely unconscious of all this.

Intent in his purpose, tranquil of mien, absorbed in his vision, he straightened up carefully, gauging his balance.

Feet apart, he steadied himself. The mayil quivered . The apples on his chest seemed to well up like blood. His yellow veshti fluttered in a sudden current.

The man who had been seated on the Azhagan's right picked up the stools and stacked them. I glimpsed his friends hazily through the shimmer of the mayil and the haze of incense smoking at a small altar. Like me, they were a galaxy away from the central figure robed in light.

On the stone flags, his shadow quivered with his steady breathing. Fascinated, I realized this shadow was the purpose of the elaborate construction. Together, the gopuram, the mayil and the Azhagan composed the shadow on the ground, the outline of a peacock.

And with every twitch and shudder of the peacock, a presence gathered in the courtyard. The stacked plastic stools, the watching company, the scatter of objects at the altar, these, the temporal and tangible, were part of the incarnation of the ancient and invisible. Without them, he would have been merely a bizarre apparition. But with these mundane satellites he gained majesty. He was no longer a man in a steel cage, pierced and pinioned and weighed down. He was aerial, skimming the ground, a bird, a god, a hope, a poem.

Arohara! The crowd exclaimed in a hushed whisper, quickly stifled by the Azhagan's stillness into a wondering silence.

All at once that peace was startled.

The gleaming mayil trembled, but he quickly regained balance.

But we had noticed, before we registered what had startled him.

A short sharp scream. And here it came again.

The scream made us all turn in that direction, forgetting him.

A woman had fallen to the ground, writhing in convulsions. She was ordinarily clad, not in a celebrant's yellow. Her grey hair had come loose from its knot and lashed like a lithe snake as her head tossed this way and that.

People crowded around her. Shukla and Shaktivel hurried down to investigate.

I turned away.

The Mayil Azhagan stood resplendent in a patch of sunlight. His friends had departed, except for one young man. The trellis of the mayil, decorated with jasmine, glittered in the sun.

The Mayil Azhagan's eyes were stern with the concentration of keeping his vel steady. His hands held the bamboo rods lightly.

The silken drapery of his gold-bordered yellow veshti filtered the sunlight. At his feet, the peacock's shadow breathed and shifted.

He seemed to gain in stature as he advanced slowly into the centre of the sunlit yard, a peacock quivering and ready for flight.

Murugan the Beautiful had arrived.

I never got a chance to tell Lalli about Ambarnath. When I reached home, I found her ill. I gave her a bit of the delectable kai murukku Shukla had acquired somehow, but said nothing of what I had seen. In the anxious month that followed, I had almost forgotten that day trip myself.

Now, as I told Lalli the story, the day returned in synesthetic detail.

Lalli had heard my account eagerly, but her listless smile told me she had found nothing suggestive of her memory. Still, the diversion helped. We had a cheery breakfast in the balcony, talking banalities till we returned, inevitably, to the case at hand.

Savio had questioned Subbu Bhagavathar last evening. He hadn't done any better than Shaktivel. Savio had not mentioned the advent of Guru.

Subbu Bhagavathar was likely to be discharged this morning, but Savio had asked the hospital to hold on till Forensics were done with the crime scene.

'There's always something they rush back for,' he grumbled. 'Remember the time they wanted more bloodstains a fortnight after the murder?'

'Anyway Subbu will be looking for new lodgings,' I said. 'The temple won't help now, either. No brother, no son, no job, no roof and probably no money. He'll welcome Guru with open arms.'

'Quite the cynic, aren't you?'

Lalli and I were at Sion Hospital soon after breakfast. We found Subbu Bhagavathar waiting for us in an anteroom outside Neurosurgery. The constable seated nearby greeted Lalli with a broad smile.

'Khobragade, isn't it? How's the foot?'

'Good as new. Your daughter?'

'My niece.'

'Your aunt is the reason I'm alive today. Look after her.' He scribbled something on his folded newspaper and tore off the strip. 'Keep my mobile number. Anything you need, anytime.'

As he handed me the slip of paper, I was surprised to see his eyes were bright with tears. I wondered what kind of mess Lalli had rescued him from.

Subbu Bhagavathar still wore the surly look I had noticed in Shaktivel's video.

'Who are you?' he greeted Lalli in Marathi.

'My name is Lalli. I work with the police. I'm here to talk about your son,' Lalli replied in Tamil.

'My good fortune!' His face relaxed. 'I can speak freely with you and hope to be understood.'

'Certainly. How are you feeling this morning? Is the headache still bad?'

'Headache? I've lost my head completely in the last few hours. My friend is dead. My brother is dead. My son is a murderer. My head itself is missing—I'm walking around like Bhakta Kumanan. You know that story, don't you?'

Lalli hastily intercepted the imminent Harikatha by saying, 'Oh yes, he brought his own head on a plate as offering. I hope you will be spared that fate. But let's get down to details.'

'What can I tell you?'

'When did Senthil lose his mother?'

'When he was...about seven. She got high fever and died within a few hours.'

'In hospital?'

'No—yes, you could say that, maybe. She died in the taxi on the way to hospital. They wouldn't admit her, saying she was dead already. It was terrible. I performed the rites from hospital itself, taking the body to the crematorium, so that the children would not be upset. Oh, why did you remind me of that day?'

'When did Senthil first get fits?'

'Soon after. I realized the boy was grieving for his mother. He was not fit for school. I decided to teach him myself. He was not good at studies, but he was good at memorizing, so I taught him all I know. By the age of ten he was singing Thevaram as though he was born to it. I started taking him along with me when I performed Harikatha. He had fits frequently. I decided this was the only suitable life for him. He is twenty-five now, and look what he has done. I did my best to give him a good life—a holy life, and look what he's done.'

'You seem certain of his guilt.'

'The policeman I spoke to, young fellow, speaks a little Tamil, he didn't tell me his name—'

'Sub-Inspector Shaktivel.'

'Shaktivel? Then he is pakka Tamilian, why can't

he speak the language properly? Education, you call this? Anyway, this Shaktivel showed me some photos—Sivasiva! My son Senthil, covered with blood, staring like a madman, my brother's body, his head smashed with a pestle! What is left for me to say, Amma? You better see those photos.'

'I have seen them.'

'And yet you ask if my son is guilty? Yes, he is guilty. Do I think he's guilty? No. Why not? Because he is an innocent. He doesn't know what he's doing immediately after a fit. Sometimes he wanders off. Sometimes he recites poetry, but he always has a wild look, and can never remember what he's done afterwards.'

'So what do you think he deserves now?'

'A murderer deserves to hang. But he is my son. I want him to live. But in prison? What will happen to this innocent in jail? He won't know what's happening. He'll go wild. He may kill again. I've been thinking about this ever since I saw those photos. I wish he would die. I want you to hang him. It will be most merciful.'

He folded his hands on his considerable stomach and nodded in resignation.

'What about medical treatment? Perhaps that's what he needs now, hospital instead of prison.'

'No use. He's had medical treatment. In this very hospital they made him a mental case and put him in Thana asylum for six months. He was so unhappy.

I couldn't bear it. I took him home against the doctors' advice. Whatever he may be, he's my son, I told them, mad or sane, I'll take care of him. But I was wrong, wasn't I? I should have kept him there, and averted this sin.'

'You have asked to see him, haven't you?'

'Of course, I must see him as soon as possible. He must have his medicine too. I have that at home. I have to prepare a kashayam.'

'How do you prepare that?'

'A vaidyan, very famous vaidyan, gives me the powder every year, and I boil it and make a kashayam. It makes Senthil sleep peacefully for a few hours. When he wakes, the headache is gone.'

'What will you do now?'

'I don't know. First, I need my bag. Will you tell Inspector Shaktivel to please restore it to me? He tells me he has recovered it. It contains all the things I need for my work—panchangam, darbha, books, that sort of thing.'

'I'll tell him, although it will be a while before you get back to work. Meanwhile, where will you go when you're discharged from hospital? Your house is a crime scene and you won't be allowed in.'

'I never want to step into that house again! Besides, I'm sure the landlord will make trouble. Nobody wants a tenant who has caused a scandal. The temple will let me sleep there, I hope. You are right, my job is done with now. How will they call me for Harikatha knowing my son is a rogue?

Senthil has murdered more than my brother! He has murdered his own father too! I have led a blameless life, how have I deserved this?'

Lalli could not disguise her distaste. There was a sharp edge to her voice as she demanded, 'What about your other son?'

He stared at her, nonplussed. After a few minutes, he growled, 'What other son? Senthil is my only child.'

'I'm talking of the son who ran away.' Lalli paused. When he continued to stare at her, she said, 'Guru. Kumaraguru, right?'

He uttered a cry of outrage and buried his face in his hands.

'Enough! Enough! Have I not suffered enough? Why bring up that tragedy now? I searched the whole world for that boy—he was Senthil's twin—he ran away frightened by Senthil's fits. And then who knows what happened? Somebody kidnapped him. Killed him, sold him, made a slave of him maybe—Who can tell? For a whole year I walked up and down the city, asked here, asked there. No use. Nobody could find him.'

'You made a police complaint?'

'Oh! Don't ask. Wife dead, one son sick, another lost, and police on top of all that? Please, I don't want to talk anymore, it's too much, too much!'

'You'll be happy to hear Guru is well and thriving.'

'What? My Guru?'

'So it appears. He met your brother—'

'Narayanan? He met Narayanan? Oh, that Senthil should slaughter him before he gave me the good news!'

Unfazed by this ridiculous exclamation, Lalli demanded, 'Do you think Senthil killed him because he brought this news?'

'Siva, siva, what a terrible thought! No, no, Senthil may have killed my brother, but believe me, he didn't know what he was doing.'

'We will be conducting medical tests on Senthil.'

'I will not allow that. They may harm him.'

'They may save him from the noose.'

'And ensure what? A lifetime in the asylum? What would you do if he were your son?'

'I would give him a chance to live.'

'Is that any kind of life?'

'Senthil must decide.'

'How can he decide? He is mentally ill. I am his guardian. That is the law.'

'Really? We'll see about that.'

Lalli rose abruptly and walked out.

'Hot-tempered lady,' Subbu Bhagavathar observed. 'I was told some hotshot detective is coming. This is just an old Mami.'

'An old Mami who will shake the truth out of you, old man,' I replied as I left.

Lalli was thoughtful on the way out. 'Perhaps it will make things worse all around if Subbu meets Senthil now.'

'I agree he's awful, but he's Senthil's father, Lalli!'

'Didn't behave like one, did he? Move over, I'm driving.'

That meant destination unknown.

It's always slightly maddening, and madly exciting, when Lalli takes the wheel. She drives like the devil's grandmother, overtaking every vehicle on the road by sheer bloody-minded intent. No speeding, but such tenacity that she won't concede one millimeter of road.

Sometimes there's the excitement of not knowing where we're headed. At other times the destination's plain, but the route unexpected, threading through parts of the city I never knew existed.

Today she took the Sixty-foot Road, headed into Mahim, and parked opposite an old building just beyond the station.

'I hope we haven't come to the wrong place,' she murmured. 'You know, Sita, in trying to remember, I'm forgetting just too many things.'

I followed her up the staircase, dodging drips from the roof. The balustrade had all but given way under the corrosion of time and damp. We went up to the third floor and Lalli knocked on a nondescript door.

There was a slow shuffle of feet, and the door opened to a chink.

A spectacled eye ogled us for a long moment, then the door flew open with an exclamation.

'Lalli, after all these years! Is it really you?'

The man who stood before us was nearly bent double. Head tilted painfully, he met Lalli's eyes with a laugh of pure pleasure.

'Raymond.' Lalli's voice was delighted, but she couldn't keep the stricken look from her eyes.

'Come in, come in! And your lovely friend—not daughter, no, no, tell me not your daughter.'

'Niece, Raymond.'

'Thank God. Thought for a moment you went and broke my heart one more time with some bugger.'

'Raymond, how did you let it get so bad?'

'No treatment, they told me, bamboo spine. Last two years I've given up, can't hold the instrument. Never mind, I've had my glory days. Tell me about yourself, and to what I owe this unexpected pleasure.'

He led us into an excruciatingly neat room. Everything in it was shiny and angular. The only curved surface was the violin case placed on a piece of silk on top of the pianoforte.

Through the doorway I caught a glimpse of a tiny pantry and passage.

Raymond waved us into two severe chairs and settled on the piano stool. Considering his deformity, I was surprised he had chosen that seat, but he seemed quite at ease.

Lalli came to the point at once.

'Raymond, do you remember a boy called Guru? About twelve or thirteen years ago—'

Raymond chuckled richly in answer. 'Boy? Is that what he's called these days? Bloody Heifetz, the bugger was. Luckiest day in my life, the day he pinched my violin. Lalli, have you heard him play?'

'Not yet. Good, eh?'

'Truly gifted. Privilege to hear him.'

'This is you, Raymond Gomes, the best violinist I've heard, saying this?'

'Pah. My days are long over, and they were never very good. Now, who plays the violin or the piano? Everything's electronic. I told the boy, get out. Get out, I said and find out what you can do, I've taught you all I know. So where did you meet him?' Raymond narrowed his eyes, making his spectacles jump. 'Trouble? Wild boy, quick-tempered, but basically honest and good-hearted. Made him take the Trinity, but I don't think he finished. Had to work, no? You know he was a runaway kid when I met him, chokra in the college canteen.'

'He told me.'

'When he played with me one Christmas, the Fathers offered to educate him, give him a home in the orphanage, but I told him—avoid. Be hungry, but stay free. Used to sleep on the landing here for four-five years, then he got a place in a factory. Cleared his SSC. Studying was no problem for him. Get out, I told him, don't let life bugger you the way it's buggered me. Truth is, long before my spine became bamboo, I was bambooed through and through.'

'Still teach, don't you?'

'Those who can't, teach.'

'I've never believed that.'

'Get the boy to play for you. You've got a good ear, Lalli.'

'Would you like to come listen to him? I've asked him to play Paganini.'

'Bad girl, you.'

'I saw his hands, Raymond.'

'Capriccio 24. Ask him for that.'

'Ask him yourself. Give me your number.'

'Okay, but I don't travel,' he shrugged, embarrassed.

'Oh, you will!'

We took our leave. As we got into the car, Lalli said, 'I wish I'd looked him up earlier.'

'Did he teach you music?'

'Oh no, no, I've never learnt—'

She didn't finish the sentence.

Something had her transfixed. A moment later as she started the car, I noticed the flush, the air of expectancy.

'You always put me back on track, Sita.' She gave me an unexpected hug.

'So he did teach you music?'

'Eh? Who? Oh, Raymond? No, no, Raymond taught me the tango.'

The tango!

I'd kill to be able to dance a tango, but my musical inabilities extend to dance as well.

But she had remembered something else—something musical again.

By the time we had both these murders solved, I would be a wreck. Toaddly, as Shukla would put it.

I expected to go home, but Lalli drove to the mortuary. Dr Q would be elbow deep in cadavers at this hour.

Did Lalli mean to attend the autopsy on Narayanan?

Reading my thought, she said, 'I asked Savio to meet us here, let's go to Dr Q's office.'

Dr Q occupies a semi-circular room in the stone building of the old Coroner's Court. That isn't as grand as it sounds. It's small, cramped, and crowded with curiosae. The desk is standard issue, circa 1960, massive and immovable, with a useless writing surface of faded green felt decorated with ballpoint squiggles and ink stains that Dr Q has warred against for a lifetime.

The sole object of veneration on that desk is his bag. It looks like a truant from some fabulous bestiary, a chimera that has crawled up and died. Part dragon, part rhino, with an ancestral whiff of buffalo, I'd say. It's scaly, bulges in a belligerently armoured sort of way, and is the exact shade of a buffalo wallowing in a bog. The strap, long and alarmingly tensile despite its craquelure, could be mistaken for a pangolin's tail. The bag's interior, though, is utterly professional, and completely in keeping with Dr Q's persuasion. It is lined with fabric that has the colour and texture of fresh cerement. Its cavity is divided by a pinkish grey diaphragm that Dr Q assures me is watered silk, but it has, in fact, the slithery feel of a sheet of muscle. The two principal caverns have membranous pockets which contain portable memorabilia: a fragment of skull, a mummified finger, the odd molar or two.

There are always books, and no matter what they looked like on the shelf, once in the bag they immediately acquire the wrinkled immortality of pickled body parts.

An easy transformation, really, as most of Dr Q's treasures are leather-bound or cloth-covered tomes, the more obscure and antique rejects of libraries, raddi shops and pavement stalls.

I've seen him extract a precious copy of *Utopia,* practically indistinguishable from a spleen.

Nobody's permitted to touch this bag. Dr Q's silent displeasure can be painfully abrasive.

Yet today Lalli appropriated the bag the moment she entered the room. To say I was aghast would be an understatement.

She opened the bag and took out a book—a leather folder, actually—and slipped it into her own bag. She gave me no explanation and I couldn't rid myself of the thought that there was something faintly surreptitious about her action.

Savio chose just that moment to come in, and the warning look in Lalli's eye explained everything. Whatever the folder contained, it had to do with Lalli's own quest.

'Lalli, the kid's legit, everything checks out.' Savio slid into a chair, stretching out his legs. 'God, I've been so cramped all morning. I've taken the afternoon off to play football.'

'I'd love to see Shaktivel's face when he hears that,' Lalli smiled.

'I can't understand Shukla's weakness for him,' I said.

'Tenacity,' both of them answered.

'Eh?'

'He won't let go till he's found what he's looking for,' Savio spelt it out for me.

'All his reasoning is faulty, but he's a bloodhound,' Lalli added.

'Brilliant but no brain,' I capped it with Shukla's own appraisal. 'What's he up to now?'

'Background check on Subbu Bhagavathar. What did you think of Subbu, Lalli?'

'Definitely not to the manner born.'

'How can you say that, Lalli?' I protested. 'He was so theatrical.'

'Exactly. He was a caricature, not the real thing.'

'You mean he's not a Harikatha guy?' Savio asked. 'But he's well-known. A bit boring, the temple fellows told me, they've seen better, but sound. And Senthil, apparently, is a great hit when he sings.'

'Easy to say he's boring now that they don't want him back,' I remarked.

'No, then they would have dissed Senthil's singing,' Savio pointed out. 'They're horrified by his crime. When I threw them the suggestion that his epilepsy may have been responsible, there were no takers. "We've witnessed his fits very often, especially this year, but he usually fell asleep immediately thereafter. We've never seen him do anything automatically," I was told.'

'I think they were speaking the truth when they said Subbu's Harikatha was boring,' Lalli said. 'It's a performance art that relies on irony and humour as much as it does on lore and music. A Bhagavathar generally engages the audience through witty parallels between myth and daily life, and you can't do that without humour. Subbu's lacking that ingredient.'

'So maybe he's just a poor performer,' I said. 'From your comment I imagined you thought him an imposter.'

Lalli laughed. She has this ringing dangerous laugh that bodes very ill for her prey—but there was no prey in sight this time. It left me puzzled.

'Lalli, I've given Guru permission to visit Senthil at four o'clock. Could you sit in?'

'No, I'm afraid not. I'll have a quick word with Dr Q and then I must run. Sita can sit in, though.'

'Me?'

'Yeah, why not. Senthil speaks a comfortable

mix of English, Hindi and Marathi, but that's very superficial. It's only in Tamil that he'll reveal himself.'

'Guru doesn't speak Tamil,' I pointed out.

'Exactly,' they chorused.

Dr Q arrived, looking even more dapper than usual. He's always dressed in pristine white. Looking at him you'd never guess he's been mucking about in gore.

He raised his left eyebrow at Lalli, and she nodded ever so faintly.

'A redundant autopsy,' Dr Q said. 'Besides confirming what's self-evident, I found nothing of interest in the late Mr Narayanan. The victim was a healthy sixty-five, no "lifestyle diseases". Speaks highly of his lifestyle, if you ask me. Shukla showed me the interview with his brother—I suppose all the lifestyle illnesses fell to his share. What's all this I hear about a twin?'

'Sita's going to sit in on the meeting between the brothers. I wish you'd go with her, Dr Q,' Lalli surprised me by saying.

'I? What would I do there? They'll speak in Tamil and I don't know the language.'

'But Sita does. I need you for the other language.'

'Ah.'

'What other language?' I asked.

Savio smiled. 'The one without words,' he said.

'Am I, really?' I railed as Dr Q drove to Sion.

Lalli had taken the Fiat, Savio was off playing

football, and Dr Q was a captive target for my indignation.

'Really what? Oh. Bad at the other language? Gain some, lose some, Sita.'

That was a terrible judgment on a writer. I was close to tears.

'I wouldn't be so hard on myself if I were you,' Dr Q said. 'You are a word child, though.'

'And you're not?'

'No. I read, yes, but my thoughts are not verbal.'

'What are they, then?'

'I've often wondered, but I can't tell. I'm not like you, and I'm not like Ramachandran. He thinks in music.'

'That's not possible.'

'Of course it is. I'm not talking about how he explained the emotion of a song yesterday. He was able to evoke a memory in Lalli. How did he do that? How did he know what to sing? The other *raags* were beautiful too, but he chose this one.'

'I think it was the emotion it evoked. It's a very haunting melody.'

'So you think Lalli remembered an emotion? Not an event?'

'I don't know,' I lied.

Lalli had reported something much more complicated: that last song had brought up the memory of another, and she couldn't remember what that was.

I thought despairingly of an infinite regression of musical notes in a room full of mirrors.

And suddenly I realized that's what Lalli must be hearing every waking moment, and possibly in her dreams. Even Noriega, bombarded with heavy metal, couldn't have been tormented as much. I returned to the argument.

'Ramachandran says Senthil's true reality is myth. You, Dr Q, say his true reality is music. Mine is words. And you don't know what your reality is—'

'If by reality you mean thought, yes.'

'Then how do we understand each other? And how on earth am I going to help Lalli if I have nothing else but words?'

'Oh, you will. When Lalli said sit in, did she mean us to be actually in the room when the brothers meet?'

'No, I think they'll be in the rat chamber, and we'll take the cat.'

'What on earth do you mean?'

I explained.

'This sounds as though it's part of Shukla's project,' Dr Q smiled.

'What is this project all about? He's embarrassed as hell about it, and Shaktivel's all cocky.'

'Look, there it is.'

'What? Where?'

'Just ahead, to your left.'

Dr Q gestured towards a large billboard which read BE AWARE OF BOGUS POLICE.

'That's Shukla's project?' I asked incredulously.

'And the traffic signs. Have you noticed those?'

I had, actually.

IF YOU DRIVE WITHOUT A SENSE,
YOU WILL BE IN AMBULANCE.

WEAR BELT, SAVE LIFE.

BECAUSE YOU BORN, THINK OF MOTHER,
BEFORE YOU HORN, THINK OF OTHER.

SKIDDING IN HEAVY RAIN?
WEAR HELMET, SAVE BRAIN.

SPEED BRINGS END TO LIFE
PLEASE CARE FOR CHILDREN AND WIFE.

And the more menacing:
VALUE LIFE, THINK OF WIFE.

They were all more Shaktivel than Shukla.

'It started because of the *Aapghat kshetra* signs,' Dr Q said. 'Shukla made a formal complaint after the number of road accidents increased at such points. His complaint letter was very simple. *Aapghat kshetra: What it means? Nobody knows. In very process of finding out, they are in kshetra without knowledge and aapghat is over. Road sign must be understood by driver.*'

It was a letter nobody could ignore.

A meeting was called hastily. Dr Q was summoned to brief them on the nature of injuries.

Aapghat kshetra was jettisoned.

The commissioner suggested DANGER AHEAD with an icon.

Shukla agreed, but Shaktivel, who had accompanied Shukla, objected.

'What is A HEAD?' he demanded. 'Some people will read it as one head. If you translate it will be insult having opposite effect.'

The commissioner had asked him to explain, and Shaktivel had translated it as *Danger, tera sir* to general applause. The meeting had ended with Shukla being put in charge, with Shaktivel as deputy, to revise all road signs.

'Nobody is understanding good English,' Shukla had explained earnestly. 'Everybody is understanding bad English. Everybody is repeating bad English if it is poetry.'

'If I mention, don't take tension,' Shaktivel had offered.

If I hadn't seen Shaktivel in action I might have accused Dr Q of joking.

'Don't breathe a word of this to Shukla, please,' Dr Q smiled. 'He's terrified of you.'

'Of me?'

'Well, of your cooking, mostly.'

I laughed. 'Did I tell you? We're allies on Lalli's matter. He calls it dentating.'

'What? Ah. Détente.'

Still, Shukla's gleaming dentition lit up the porch as we parked.

'Cat chamber is waiting, rat chamber is ready,' he chanted happily. 'So PM over on Narayanan, Dr Q? Bheja masala?'

'Complete.'

'Irony. You're knowing irony, I think, Sita? It is poetic device. In life, pure vegetarian. In death, bheja masala. Irony, pure and simple.'

Guru hadn't yet arrived.

I asked Shukla if Senthil knew he was about to meet his twin.

'Better you tell him, Sita. Please. Boy has been sitting like a statue since then, won't touch food or water, doesn't answer questions. I will have him brought.'

I entered the rat chamber with some trepidation.

Luckily the window stood open today and Shukla didn't switch on the AC.

Senthil was brought in by his usual escort. He gestured at them to stay. Oddly, their presence seemed to reassure him. He looked dull and apathetic. He addressed me in an exhausted whisper, 'Where's the other lady? Won't she come to see me?'

'She will, very soon. Senthil, have you eaten this morning?'

'I'm not hungry. I'll eat when I get home.'

'That might take a while, you do know that, don't you?'

'Yes, I do. My father is in hospital. He's had an accident. They said his skull is broken. Will you take me to him? Is his condition serious?'

'I've just spoken with your father. His injuries were minor. All he needs is some more rest in hospital, and he's going to be all right.'

'Does he know about all this?'

'Yes.'

'Does he believe me innocent?'

I hesitated. As I began to speak, he stopped me with an imperious gesture. 'Don't bother to lie. I know what he must have said. He thinks I'm mad. He thinks I'm capable of evil when I have a fit. He's certainly seen me—and I can't see myself when I have a seizure. Maybe he's right. But I know, I know I have not done this.'

'Senthil, I'm here on another matter.'

'Can there be any other matter for me right now?'

'There is. Do you remember your brother?'

'What brother?'

'Your twin brother.'

'I don't have a twin brother.'

'Senthil, you do. He ran away when you were seven. Guru.'

'Guru!' he exclaimed in amazement. 'Guru!'

'You do remember, then?'

'Only the name. Guru!'

His voice grew increasingly infantile as he called out the name. I reached for his hand to calm him. His fingers entrapped mine in a vice-like grip that made me cry out in pain. He released me in alarm.

'Forgive me. I have answered your kindness by inflicting pain, please forgive me.'

I assured him it was nothing.

In a more rational voice, he asked, 'Maybe I had a brother once. I don't remember him, but the name is dear to me. It comforts me.'

'Senthil, your brother is here.'

'Here? What do you mean? Have you put him in jail too? Is he a criminal?'

'No. He met your chittappa last week. He went to your house yesterday, and learned what had happened. He wants to meet you.'

'Has he met my father?'

'No. He doesn't want to.'

'Where's he been hiding all these years? What does he look like? What have you told him about me? That I'm a murderer?'

'He knows you've been arrested for the murder of your chittappa.'

'So he's coming here to see what a murderer looks like.'

'No. He's coming here to see what his brother looks like.'

'Guru. Guru.' He whispered the name thoughtfully.

My phone rang just then.

It was Lalli. I hurried out to take the call.

As I passed the foyer, I caught sight of Guru. He was waiting in a corner, clutching his violin case. He didn't see me, though I walked right past him. The reception within the building was poor. I got out into the open and called Lalli. I told her what had just transpired.

'The boy sounds very fragile,' Lalli said worriedly.

'He's intent on starving till he gets home.'

'Oh, nonsense, we'll get him out of that. Apparently Subbu Bhagavathar is on the lam. He sneaked off right under the constable's nose. He's very likely to turn up there, Sita. You're in for a long session.'

'Guru's here already. I saw him waiting for Shukla.'

'Oh good. I wanted them to meet before Subbu got there.'

'It's likely to be quite a reunion. Guru's brought his violin.'

I heard a sharp intake of breath. 'Stop him, Sita!'

'Eh?'

'Stop Guru from playing—don't waste time, run!'

I ran.

Guru was no longer in his corner.

Presumably, Shukla had conducted him already into the rat chamber. I hurried in that direction, and was surprised to see Dr Q disappear into that very room.

I was too late.

Senthil had collapsed, convulsing uncontrollably while Guru, violin in hand, stared on in horror.

Senthil's seizure lasted for about ten minutes, leaving him inert. Dr Q insisted on hospitalizing him immediately—and under his own supervision.

I was relieved Senthil wasn't being taken to Sion Hospital. His past experience there had led to a six-month incarceration in an asylum. Whatever ailed Senthil's brain, it was not insanity. Even I could tell that.

'I thought I'd enter playing that old tune, hoping it would make him remember,' Guru said miserably. 'He started shaking the moment I entered. Almost as if I had brought on the fit.'

'You shouldn't blame yourself,' I said absently.

'But that's exactly what happened,' Dr Q told me a few minutes later as we stepped out together. 'I was in Shukla's cat chamber, observing the boy. After you left, he was muttering to himself, shaking his head and smiling. He looked excited. Then I heard music. It sounded like a violin, a lilting tune. I idly wondered where it was coming from—but I was distracted by the dramatic change in the boy. He rose, wringing his hands and whimpering. His face was a grimace of terror. The next moment, he had started convulsing. I rushed here. Just as I left the cat room, I caught a glimpse of Guru entering playing his violin. Ah, here comes the ambulance—'

Dr Q hurried away.

I felt dizzy. I had stumbled on a discovery so impossible that I was almost unwilling to face it. It was wild, irrational, utterly implausible—but it was a moment of self-discovery and therefore undeniable.

I tried calling Lalli, but she was out of range. Savio

too was not contactable. Shukla had accompanied Senthil.

Dr Q had followed the ambulance, leaving me to pick my way home. Guru had left too and I didn't expect to see him again.

I was alone, electric with discovery. There was just one more fact I needed to make my discovery water-tight.

I rang Ramachandran's number.

He picked up almost at once.

'Sita! What's happened? Are you all right?'

The anxiety in his tone surprised me. How could he possibly know something had happened? I said nothing about Senthil's seizure. Instead I asked, without preamble, 'Were you singing when Senthil rang your doorbell the first time? It was Ganesh Chathurthi, right?'

'Yes.' His voice trailed off. 'Got it, Sita. Yes, Ponni had just finished singing *Sri Ganapatini* in Saurashtram. You know the song?'

'Sort of, yes.'

'I remember she did a beautiful *niraval* on the greedy line—*panasa narikela jambu*...' and he began to hum it infuriatingly. Would he never get to the point?

'Sorry, I was carried away. It was really a very good *niraval*. Yes, I sang after that, something small and simple. *Siddhi Vinayakam*, I think. Why?'

'Tell you later, sorry to have barged in on you like this.' I rang off.

I felt ill. My mouth was dry, the percussionist within my ribs was spinning out of control. I was blacking out.

I sank down on a bench, giving in to the clangour in my skull. My head was exploding with music, notes that whirled up in a tsunami of sound, building up an unbearable tension as they hammered for escape—

'Sita.'

Lalli's voice broke past the roar of music.

I felt her hand rest gently on my head. Under her soothing fingers the tidal rush began to ebb.

'Let's go home.'

She put her arm around me and walked me to the car. Her embrace, usually so strong and resilient, was light as a moth's wing. Shame stung me, making me irritable.

'I'm driving.'

She handed me the keys.

'Too late, were you?' she asked as I started the car.

'Yeah. Your Paganini entered playing *Shyamale meenakshi* and Senthil erupted in fits. Dr Q's taken him to hospital, planning to admit him in Neurology.'

'Oh, good. I didn't want him sucked into the system at Sion, and sent back to the asylum. Now Savio can investigate him too.'

She had missed the point, hadn't she?

'Lalli, don't you see it?' I cried out. 'How can you not? Can't you see what's happening to Senthil?'

'Pull over, and tell me what's on your mind, Sita.'

'Let's get home.'

'No. Now.'

I obeyed. It had to be said some time, but now that I was about to, it sounded simply crazy.

'Say it, just say it.'

I took a deep breath and said it.

'Senthil has a fit every time he hears a Dikshitar *kriti*.'

Lalli didn't respond.

I elaborated. 'All three instances were brought on just like that. I spoke with Ramachandran. The day Senthil had a fit on his doorstep, Ramachandran was singing *Siddhi Vinayakam* when Ponni got the door. And his sonorous voice would have resounded past that door long before. That's the first time. The second was with *Kadambari priyai* and now with *Shyamale meenakshi*.'

Lalli continued to regard me with calm expectation.

'Wait. You anticipated this?' I gasped. 'Is that why you asked me to stop Guru from playing?'

Lalli nodded. 'I didn't look at it from your point of view, though.'

'You expected him to play *Shyamale meenakshi*, didn't you? The tune might bring up painful memories, as it did for Guru, and pain might bring on a convulsion.'

'Yes.'

'So we're right?'

'Savio's not likely to finish his game before six, so let's leave it till tomorrow. By then we should have heard from Dr Q.'

Lalli was busy in her room all evening, leaving me to my simmering thoughts. Unable to bring them to a boil, I went in search of Ramachandran. He was deep in a book and didn't take kindly to the interruption. It was Mandelslo's *Travels in Western India*, a book I had long coveted. We stared at each other in polite antagonism for a while. Then he said, 'Okay, Sita, what's on your mind?'

'Senthil has a fit if he hears a Dikshitar *kriti*.'

'So I gathered from your phone call. The brother arrived with *Shyamale meenakshi* on his fiddle, I suppose?'

'Yes. What do you know about—er?'

'Er? About the toxic effects of Dikshitar? Leave the poor man out of this, Sita. He led a blameless life.'

'How do you know? Is there any legend of his about having cured diseases with his music?'

'Surely you mean induced diseases, not cured?'

'Cured. The others wouldn't be celebrated as legend.'

'There's the usual load of rubbish churned up every season. May have been more if he'd lived earlier, but Dikshitar was just yesterday. Myth needs at least five hundred years to solidify as history. But—' He paused.

I was afraid to prompt. I picked up Mandelslo and leafed through it idly.

He deftly plucked the book from my fingers. 'There's the other possibility—two, in fact. First, the *raagam* and not the *kriti* brought about the convulsion. Ponni's friend Aparna Desai works on the effects of music on the body. You could talk to her.'

'You don't sound as if you have much faith in that.'

'I don't. There's no objectivity in it. Different *raagams* induce different emotions in different people. One that induces melancholy in me might make you joyous. It depends on the emotion the singer projects. The body responds to the emotion, not to the *raagam*.'

'You're very prosaic for a musician.'

'I'm not a musician. I sing a little, this and that, and not very well. And I hate mystifying music. It's probably the most primitive human experience. You can't make mumbo jumbo out of that.'

'But that's what makes classical music, surely?'

He laughed. 'A *raagam* is just a blueprint for the sounds of a particular region or tribe. The sound memory of a culture, a language. Maybe two thousand years on people will be singing a Vile Parle *raagam* as we sing Kambodhi or Saurashtram.'

'What about using music to cure diseases?'

'Sure. Aparna says I can cure my diabetes with Bageshri. Someday I'll eat a bowl of halwa and test that out.' He brushed away the thought with contempt.

'What's the other possibility?' I asked.

'Oh, that? Take the Mandelslo if you want it so badly, Sita.'

I knew there was nothing more to be got out of him.

'I don't want the book.'

'Right.'

'If you wanted to explain Senthil's predicament now, his emotions at this moment, what song would you choose?'

'How can I presume, Sita? I'm not Senthil.'

'Still. I'd like you to try, please. He's just had a bad convulsion. He may be asleep. He will wake soon to a slow realization of what's happening to him. I want to hear that moment.'

He considered that, then surprised me by breaking into a lovely *thillana*, delicate as the lyric that followed *Va velava, vadivelava mayilmeedu ni va...*[5]

'This myth, this fairy tale is Senthil's reality,' Ramachandran said. 'But soon, the reality forced on him will have to be faced. I'll sing that reality now.'

5. Come, O holder of the vel, ride in on your peacock.

This was a more predictable choice. Tyagaraja's child-like tantrum in Reethigowla, *Nannu vidachi kadalakura*. The heart-rending lyric has wheedle and threat in perfect equipoise; *not for half a moment can I bear to be separated from you, do not abandon me now!*

'Well? And how does that help you?' he demanded, his rumbling baritone jolting me back to the mundane.

'Oh, it's helped more than you know. It's told me what you refused to, a few minutes ago.'

And leaving him with that irritating thought, I went home.

'Lalli, I think I know what's happening to Senthil,' I announced.

Savio, happily demolishing a stack of parathas, nodded encouragingly. 'Tell us now, I'm wiring him up in the morning.'

'Can we come?'

'You have to ask?'

'I learned to look at this music thing differently today,' I began. 'It started with you telling me I was no good at the language without words—'

'Oh God, Lalli! She'll whip us with that for the rest of our lives,' Savio groaned.

Lalli laughed. 'We can always get back wordlessly.'

'Oh don't worry, you didn't break my heart, but it got me thinking. I think in words. Dr Q says Ramachandran thinks in music. Senthil thinks in myth. Everybody has a language of thought. Ramachandran said there are two possibilities for why Senthil has a fit when he hears a Dikshitar *kriti*. First—the emotion it evokes triggers the fit. The second possibility Ramachandran wouldn't talk about, but I think he means the innate music trapped within us all, the tumultous surge of excitement or else tranquillity.'

'Isn't that the same as emotion?' Savio asked.

'No. I think Sita means something more torrential—almost a change in the plane of consciousness.'

'A change in neuronal excitability?'

'Savio, I don't know what that means. But if you're going to wire him up, you'll find out.'

'Wait, I'm not done yet. That's what Ramachandran thinks. But I think Senthil has two languages of thought. Myth is his comfortable and familiar language. But Dikshitar's music is the other, the dangerous one. It's the forbidden language, the one he secretly craves. So why is it forbidden?'

'Brava!' Lalli was more than delighted.

'I think his father banned Dikshitar's music for some reason—remember Ramachandran told us Senthil said it would make his father angry to know the song had brought on a fit. Perhaps Senthil meant that particular song would make his father angry.'

'We'll ask Senthil's father tomorrow, he's got to

give consent for brain fingerprinting. Shaktivel's tracking him down.'

'Didn't turn up at the chowki?'

'Nope. Seems to have disappeared. Guru turned up at the hospital, though.'

'He did?' I was surprised. Guru had lost no time in leaving the chowki.

'Yes, he said he'd stay the night, violin and all. He's keeping out of Senthil's way at present. "I'll go in when he asks for me," he said. So our violinist is lodged in the corridor, along with the two constables guarding Senthil.'

'So Shukla finally removed Senthil's handcuffs?' I asked.

'Not at all.'

'Why does he need two constables to guard him if he's still shackled?'

'Because,' said Lalli.

'Shukla's call,' said Savio.

Lalli hadn't heard of Shukla's project, so the day ended with laughter as we pooled in bizarre additions to Shukla's wit.

None of our contributions matched the traffic signs we encountered the next morning on the highway.

LANECUTTING IS LIFECUTTING said the prickle of red and yellow lights at the signal.

I watched, fascinated, as it changed to STOP BEFORE STOP SIGN and NO BEERING WHEN STEERING.

The lights turned green, and I caught the last one just in time:

BIKERS BEHEADED WITHOUT HELMET WILL BE FINED.

Lalli said, 'Your language of thought idea's very helpful, Sita.'

'You mean with—'

'Yes. This whole Dikshitar business has me deeply worried.'

'You think it links up in some way with your memory?'

'Yes. I know Dikshitar will reveal my murder.'

That sounded most unlike Lalli. Blind faith isn't her line. And I was more than a little sceptical about banking on a musician who had been dead for two hundred years.

'I've located the year, and the month. That folder I took from Dr Q's bag told me that.'

'Oh?'

'I always send Dr Q a postcard when I'm out of town. It's a deal we made after the Padmaraga murder. I've told you about that, haven't I?'

'No!'

'Some other time. Anyway I hadn't expected him to keep the postcards, but you know Dr Q. Nothing's trivial with him.'

'How did you know the right postcard?'

'That's just it. I don't know how, but I knew when I found it. I could hear the ocean, I felt this fear.'

'Where did you mail it from?'

'Kanyakumari. 5th October, 1995.'

'That's a start, Lalli. What does the postcard say?

'Just a line. *One can see forever here, there's no horizon.* The picture is a large coral. That postcard was mailed before it happened. Before I committed the murder.'

'But it shouldn't be difficult to find out why you were there at all, and what happened.'

'I was not on leave. I was there on a case, following a lead, and of course now I can't remember what.'

'Whom were you working with?'

'C.J. Pande. He's dead. Anyway, I wouldn't have confided in him. I loathed him.'

'And you didn't tell Dr Q?'

'Oh no.'

'Friends? Family?'

'No, Sita. I don't think I'm being very clear—I didn't know then that I had committed a murder. I only realized it now.'

'I thought you remembered it now. Realizing is quite different from remembering, isn't it?'

'Yes! Remembering recalls a long realized fact. It's only when I had this fever that I realized I had committed murder. And I know it's in some way connected to a passage of music—very likely a Dikshitar *kriti*, though I haven't yet discovered which one.'

'Worse comes to worst, you could work your way through all five hundred!'

'No, I hope to discover it today.'

'Why we are doing all this, Sita?' Shukla asked when I met him in the hospital corridor. 'For sake of law and order, or for Lalli's sake? Be frank. It is first principle of dentating.'

'Fifty-fifty, I think, Shukla.'

'For Senthil it is waste. He is hundred percent guilty. No evidence otherwise. True, he is getting fits, but so are many other criminals. Maybe insanity, but that is mere legality. Point of fact is established. He has murdered Narayanan Chacha.'

'Lalli isn't sure of that.'

Now why did I say that? She hadn't said she wasn't. But here came the supporting cast.

'Hey, here comes your brilliant friend now, hot on the path of innocence.'

Shaktivel appeared at the end of the corridor, strutting in triumph. Trotting abjectly behind him, on an invisible leash, came Subbu Bhagavathar.

'He had gone in search of Guru, sir,' Shaktivel announced, ignoring me. 'Following path of innocence I thought if one son is in jail, what a man with two sons will do? He will go to son number two. Accordingly, I went to residence of said second son, and found father but not son.'

He stepped aside for Subbu who scowled at us. 'Why have you brought me here?' he said angrily.

'Your son has fits.'

'He has fits very often.'

'We're doing his medical tests today.'

'Yes, I heard that. But what do you want of me?'

'You are his father, no?'

'Not anymore. He is a criminal. You have arrested him. He is in your custody. You take all responsibility. He dies in custody, you are responsible. He is poisoned by the tests, you are responsible. Now, you are his mai-baap.'

A long speech, rendered even longer by the disgust with which it was pronounced.

Then suddenly, as if by some remote electronic morphing, the disgust peeled away, leaving his face raw with fear.

I followed his dilated eyes. They were fixed on a slight figure standing as if installed on a carpet of sunlight.

Guru.

Sensing our attention, he walked quickly towards us. His face changed as he saw Subbu Bhagavathar.

He addressed Shukla. 'Is this man my father?'

'Guru.' Subbu Bhagavathar moved nervously forward.

Guru took a very determined step backward. Then he made a formal salutation with folded hands—and walked away.

'You see? You see?' Subbu Bhagavathar hissed. 'This is how the rascal behaves. Twenty years he hasn't seen his father and this is how he behaves. Where was he for twenty years? In the gutter. Return to the gutter then, don't pollute my gaze.'

Shukla and Shaktivel got busy calming Subbu's hysteria. Lalli had gone with Savio to set up the test. I thought I'd look in on Senthil.

As I approached the ward, I heard a mellifluous chant. Vaguely familiar, I was still too distracted by the acrimony of the last few minutes to register the words until I found myself echoing them. It was the *Kandar kavacham* I had heard at Ambarnath

Almost immediately I realized why the voice was so familiar. I turned in a rush to tell Lalli, and ran full tilt into her.

'Lalli, I've solved it!' I gasped against her shoulder. 'I can explain everything now. Senthil was at Ambarnath.'

I drained the glass of iced water a nurse brought me. My epiphany had ended in a dead faint, knocking my aunt flat on the floor. I prefer not to think of the first aid rendered energetically by Shukla and Shaktivel.

My dignity somewhat restored by the cold drink, I tried to marshall my thoughts.

'You said Senthil was at Ambarnath. Why is that so significant, Sita?'

'Because—'

My voice silenced itself.

Why?

Why did my realization that Senthil was at Ambarnath explain the murder? No, it did more than that. I had a conviction that it explained everything.

'Sita, we'll have to leave that till we get home. Come along, I want a word with Senthil.'

Senthil was just concluding the *kavacham* as we went in. He greeted Lalli with folded hands. He looked rested and calm. Perhaps that was just the makeover. His hair had been neatly combed out to facilitate the application of electrodes on his scalp. He had lost the ear studs. The barber had paid him a visit too. His tight cheeks were tattooed with scars. Once again, I felt a flash of discovery.

'Police Amma, is my father here?' Senthil's voice was that of an eager child.

'He'll meet you after the test,' I said swiftly. A lie seemed in order.

'He's here, then?'

I nodded.

He smiled. 'Now I'm ready for your test. It's not just about my fits, I know that already.'

'How?' Lalli asked.

'Who's the detective here, you or me? Why would they send for you if the test was for my fits? You're going to be watching that machine to find out if I'm innocent or guilty. I asked the tall inspector if the machine tells the truth, and he says hundred percent. Then I don't need to worry. The machine will show you the truth. My brother is here, you know? Guru. I haven't seen him yet, but he plays the violin beautifully. English tunes, but so beautiful, he was playing in the corridor. I almost die listening.' Tears spilt unchecked. 'I know it sounds completely crazy, but I think I've never been so happy in my life. If only I could see Ramachandran Mama again after the machine tells the truth, I'll be completely happy.'

Suddenly turning to me he said, 'I know you want to remind me I'm a criminal. I don't need reminding. Can we go for that test now?'

I shivered as I left the room. It was uncanny how he'd read my thought. No rationalization from Savio's Truth Machine could cancel the fact of murder, and it had been on the tip of my tongue to say so.

Savio had explained the idea behind brain fingerprinting to me earlier, but I'd never watched the process.

Senthil was entirely at ease, even joking with Savio as he helped the neurologist tape on the electrodes and set up a drip.

Lalli, Savio and the neurologist huddled at the console in the next room. I decided instead to concentrate on the screen meant for Senthil. On it would appear the 'triggers' to induce changes in brain activity. The others would monitor these changes at the console.

The show began. I had the uncomfortable feeling that my own brain was under scrutiny. Surveillance of any sort gets me ballistic, but the rest of the world seems to love a reality show.

What did Senthil feel? He was screened off from my field of vision.

The 'triggers' were random and audiovisual. Photographs of the murder scene alternated with touristy landscapes. Musical triggers ranged from Indipop and jingles to snatches of *kritis* sung by Lalli, some simple, others complex.

Fifteen minutes later, the show ended with a thud.

The screen went blank.

I ran out, colliding with the others. We rushed towards Senthil.

As though jolted by an immense charge of electricity, Senthil was wracked by seismic convulsions—they lasted perhaps a few minutes and then the drugs took control and he lapsed into a daze of quietude.

'This is more than epilepsy,' I heard the neurologist say. 'Let's get him settled. I want imaging right away.'

Lalli mumured absently to me, 'The EEG suggests Senthil might have a brain tumour.'

'Is that the cause of his fits?'

'The neurologist will think so, if the imaging shows up a tumour.'

'And you don't?'

'No.'

'You shouldn't have put him through this,' I accused. 'Why did you?'

'To find out if his seizures were epilepsy. Now it doesn't seem so.'

'Does that mean he was pretending?'

'Oh no, no!'

'What next?'

'MRI to see what we can see. Sita, go home. See if you can induce Ramachandran to come here.'

'But I have to tell you—'

'Later.'

Later meant not till dinner. Good. The day would sort itself out and leave me to my notebook.

It was past sunset when Savio came in for his usual snack. In the living room, the others milled around Shukla's iPad.

Savio looked worn out. 'I don't know what to make of it.' He sighed. 'Maybe the whole thing's a fraud.'

'Your thing?'

'Yeah. I keep thinking I'll crack it this time around, but I wonder.'

'But you get results, Savio.'

'Yes. But what do these results mean? What do they tell us about the person? I just hope I haven't pushed the kid deeper into his mess. Gosh, sometimes I think I'm as bad as neurotheologists and their God spots. Rajesh is mad about that stuff.'

'Who is Rajesh?"

'Rajesh Shah, the neuro guy. He's a neurotheologist.'

'Neurotheologist? That's an oxymoron, surely.'

'Yep, completely nuts. Senthil's God's gift to neurotheo, according to Rajesh.'

'You think Senthil's innocent.'

'Did I say so?'

'No, but you called him *the kid*.'

'Yeah, he just seems such an innocent. Perpetually turning the other cheek. Even at Shaktivel.'

'That takes some doing. Did you notice Senthil's cheeks?'

'The tattoo?'

'They're not tattoos. They're scars from piercing. I saw it done at Ambarnath. Senthil's been in a religious trance before. Rajesh can knock himself out.'

'Rajesh's joining us, by the way. Should I get some dessert?'

'No, I've got it. Hot dessert.'

'Coconutty?'

'Yep.'

He left with a happy smile.

Usually, our discussions take place in the luxurious caesura before dessert. You'd imagine our brains would be too stultified for thought, but that's when they work best. The silence of repletion is a happy one, and Lalli usually chooses this moment to bring up the tangled, the thorny, and the confused.

We broke that rule this evening, as Rajesh Shah was not staying for dinner. Savio introduced him with a straight face, as a neurotheologist interested in religious nuts.

'I don't think they should be dismissed as nuts,' the neurotheologist said. 'They just have an altered reality. I should say, a transient alternate reality.'

'Do tell us how this tumour—temporal lobe, you said?—explains Senthil's symptoms,' Lalli said.

'It's the God spot. The term's no longer popular, I know, but it's the perfect explanation. Any kind of abnormality in this part of the brain can distort reality. It can induce a state of religious ecstasy, skew time and space, and generally alter perception, and that's Senthil all over, isn't it? It can also explain this guy's criminal act and his amnesia. And his unnatural calm. I was going to say holy calm. Detachment from the world. It may alternate with euphoria.'

'So temporal lobe is nirvana?' Shukla asked.

'Nirvana's just one of many manifestations. I am certain they will all be one day mapped on the brain. Think of all the mindbenders we OD on, Shukla, from soma of the Rig Veda to Ecstasy on the street.'

'That is why Shiv is shown as charsi?' Shukla asked.

'Undoubtedly. Bliss comes in different brands.' And after some more blather of a like sort, the neurotheologist took his leave.

Savio, usually the most tolerant of mortals demanded with a scowl, 'Are we never going to eat?'

Everybody was friends after dinner, even Shaktivel, who insisted on washing up. Finally, it was time to view the results of Senthil's brain fingerprinting.

'Now, Savio, kindly clear confusion of one and all,' Shukla said, as squiggle after squiggle appeared on Savio's laptop.

'One moment—Did Subbu meet Senthil?' I asked.

'No. He said he had to arrange for his brother's last rites. We released the body this afternoon,' Savio said.

'And Guru?'

'He's with Senthil.'

All attention was now on the computer screen. Savio, excitement evident from his very restraint, selected a squiggle which looked a bit different.

'This is the P300 MERMER. Memory and Encoding Related Multifaceted Electroencephalographic Response. It turns up when the brain recognizes an object or a sound—even when the subject doesn't consciously remember it.'

He scrolled down slowly. Gradually my eye registered the distinctive squiggle every time it made a sporadic appearance.

'Now let's match this against what appeared on Senthil's screen.'

We watched spellbound as the P300 MERMER

jumped up every time a photograph of the crime scene appeared. It didn't show up with the anodyne banalities of sea and sky in intervals.

Savio stopped the show to explain a few facts. P300 MERMER only appeared in context. If Senthil had not known of the murder, P300 may not have shown up when he was confronted with the murder scene. Some kind of background information seemed necessary.

The 300 stood for 300 milliseconds—the time interval between seeing the image and appearance of the wave. Something vital happened in that interval. Thought, comprehension, cognition, while the stimulus, either sound or sight, registered as memory.

Savio took a deep breath and resumed the show. He was coming to the important bit now, his bit.

'Look at this now.' Savio indicated a segment where the P300 appeared to have replicated itself. Twin P300 squiggles, separated by a brief interval.

'This happens when the subject denies the memory,' Savio said.

'When he lies?' I asked.

'No. When he suppresses the memory.'

'So first wave means, aha, now I remember this face, but then if I don't want to remember, second wave appears to tell shut up?' Shukla exposited.

'Right. Now look at Senthil's record. The single P300s mostly follow crime scene photos. All the twinned waves you see follow a musical stimulus. Now it's over to you, Lalli.'

'Dessert, Sita?' Lalli asked.

Savio followed me to the kitchen. Elai adai is always a dicey proposition, and I unwrapped the steaming parcels of banana leaf with trepidation. Yes! They slipped off easily. The adai emerged tender and glistening, a luscious bulge of rich jackfruit showing through. I plopped one into a puddle of aromatic pradaman.

'Coconutty enough for you?' I asked.

'How can I tell with just one?'

It took three more for him to decide, leaving me to wonder how many trains of P300 twins his brain showed.

Thankfully, Shukla had no complaints with the elai adai. When it comes to food, he's a rabid rationalist.

'Before we look at Senthil's response to music, I'd like to answer Shukla's question—why are we doing this?' Lalli began.

So Shukla had asked her, too.

'Everyone here, except Shaktivel, knows that I'm in the process of solving another case, one that concerns me personally—and now, Shaktivel, you know too. The two cases have something in common: music. Knowing this, Shukla asked if brain fingerprinting was for Senthil, or was it for Lalli?'

'I did not mean—' Shukla stammered in an agony of embarrassment.

'Oh, you did. You are a conscientious officer, as is Shaktivel, and you're perfectly within your rights to question my actions. And here's my answer. Senthil's brain fingerprinting was for this case, and this case alone. It has nothing to do with my personal case. If I needed to conduct tests for that, it would be in my time, at my cost and never on a prisoner in your custody. Are we clear on that now? I withdraw my request for your help, Shukla. My personal case no longer concerns you, and I will not allude to it again.'

I filled her glass, avoiding looking in Shukla's direction. She took a sip of water and began with deliberation.

'Before the test, we knew of three episodes when Senthil had a convulsion on hearing music. As Sita pointed out, all the songs that induced his fits were Dikshitar *kritis*. Did that mean all Dikshitar *kritis* could induce fits in Senthil? And if so, why? Did it have anything to do with the murder? If Senthil indeed had no memory of the murder, and was in a post-epileptic daze, had that seizure been induced by music?

'I thought I would test that out by matching the songs with Savio's brain patterns.'

Lalli took a moment to get the recordings.

'The first two songs we tested were both Dikshitar *kritis*,' Lalli said.

They had produced no P300 wave at all on Senthil's brain fingerprint.

'So all Dikshitar songs are not giving fits,' Shukla observed.

'Or Senthil was not familiar with either,' I pointed out. The songs were both complex compositions. Lalli's favourite, *Akhilandeshwari* in Dwijavanti, and the oneiric *Neelayadakshi* in Neelambari.

Lalli played the next recording—and here came the P300 wave.

'This is not a Dikshitar *kriti*, but Senthil knew this song,' Lalli said. 'And a song in the same *raagam* had produced a fit earlier.'

'So fit is not produced by *raag*, but by lyrics?' Shukla asked.

'No, we can only say the earlier song in that *raag* produced a fit, but every song in that *raag* may not. Also, Ramachandran has told me all the songs that caused fits were in different *raags*.'

Out came Dr Q's little book. 'Mohanam, Shanmukhapriya. Shankarabharanam. Very different.'

'Inconclusive. Means nothing,' Shaktivel snapped.

'Let's look at what happens with the fourth song.'

Twinned P300 waves began to appear. As the song progressed, there were more twinned waves, at increasing intervals.

'But no convulsion as yet—'

'Knowing but denying,' Shukla intoned.

'The last song is the same song that had

brought on the very first convulsion reported by Ramachandran.' *Siddhi Vinayakam.*

Twinned P300s appeared in a burst. Then the usual rhythm resumed.

'This is the point when Senthil seized up,' Lalli said.

'Test is unreliable,' Shaktivel announced. 'Prisoner is having severe fits but no visible change in brainwaves. Maybe machine is defective. More likely test itself is useless.'

'Excellent observation, Shaktivel,' Lalli smiled, 'but your inference is wrong. Senthil had a convulsion that didn't show any change in electrical activity because it was not an epileptic fit. I had the opportunity to examine him during the convulsion and it was clear to me that this was not epilepsy.'

'Any way all this is irrelevant,' Shaktivel said quickly. 'It has nothing to do with the murder.'

'On the contrary, it has everything to do with the murder. I have a question for you, Shaktivel. Why did you think that Senthil had murdered his father?'

'Uncle, madam. Victim is uncle of accused.'

'Lalli, because you are angry, you are not telling us everything' Shukla said sadly.

'Five out of ten, Shukla. I have told you everything of relevance to this case.'

'Savio, run the recording again,' Shukla said, 'and I will show Lalli what she is not telling us.'

Savio complied. When we heard Lalli's voice

singing *Sri Saraswathi*, Shukla hit pause. 'This song, Lalli. You are not telling us about this song.'

'What about it, Shukla?'

'Why are you singing so slowly? Also last song. Why?'

'Well, why not?'

'You are not answering my question.'

'No.'

'You are refusing answer?'

'You're a detective, Shukla. Find out.'

'So do you rely on Savio's test at all?' Dr Q asked.

'In this case? No. But it does confirm my deductions.'

'Which are?'

'Merely deductions for now. I need evidence.'

'All the evidence is with us, madam. Watertight case, open and shut. All this is too much waste of time,' Shaktivel said.

'In that case, Shaktivel, I won't keep you any longer. Thank you for this very pleasant evening. Shukla, you too. Good night.'

Shukla hesitated, but he would not meet Lalli's eye, and left without a word.

Dr Q walked heavily to the book shelf and selected a book. Savio picked up the newspaper. Lalli took her customary place on the beige sofa, switched on the TV, and surfed channels. I cleared the table and waited for someone to break the silence. Nobody did, but I felt the air lighten.

'You knew all along Senthil's fits weren't epileptic, didn't you, Lalli?' Savio asked.

'Any doctor would,' Dr Q answered. 'Conversion hysteria.'

'Actually I wasn't sure until I examined him during a fit. Earlier, my diagnosis leaned towards your neurotheologist's. Savio, does the man actually call himself that?'

'Yep.'

'Amaretto, Dr Q?' I asked.

'Coffee of the Borgias? Please.'

Usually, Dr Q prefers his black, with just a sheer tendril of cyanide swirled into the crema. But tonight we needed a scintilla of luxury: small cups of exquisitely smooth coffee sweetened with a dollop of almond-flavoured cream.

Savio and I split the jammy heart of the last elai adai, but the ease of our silence was sweeter by far. I felt the tender corolla of *Kadambari priyai* unfurl in memory, drenching my brain with remembered fragrance.

'I was a little hard on Shukla,' Lalli sighed. 'And I've been making you miserable, Savio. But I can't help it, you'll have to put up with it a little longer. I'm getting close. Savio, you may have to fingerprint my brain very soon.'

'Whatever for? It's not going to resurrect your lost memory.'

'No, but once I have the facts I want them tested out on me. Dr Q and Savio, I haven't told you the nature of my problem. Sita knows about it. I may have to tell you in a few days' time, but I crave your patience till then.'

'We can wait,' Dr Q said. He gave her that rare smile that transforms his stern mask. I don't think I've seen it more than twice in all our long acquaintance.

Savio said, 'The question you asked Shaktivel is the key to this case, isn't it?'

'I think so, yes.'

'What makes you so certain, Lalli?'

'Let's look at what we've got so far. You're taking the objective approach—mine is intensely subjective. So let's ask Sita to summarize.'

I understood that more than just the facts were required of me, but I had to think this over a bit. I left them to unwind a bit more as I washed and put away the coffee cups.

'I'd like to look at this upside down—or inside out,' I began. 'Rewind eighteen years. Ordinary family, twin sons. Mother dies and—bang!—the family shatters. And scatters. It takes a murder to make them into a family again. Why?'

As I fell silent, my words seemed wildly irrelevant to the situation. The obvious explanation was: son murders uncle in either trance, insanity or malice.

'Your point of view will work only if there's motive to this murder,' Savio said. 'If Senthil has committed this when mentally compromised, we can't really ascribe motive.'

'Actually, we should,' Lalli said. 'Even the insane do not commit enormities which are without logic. It's just a different logic—Shakespeare says it so much better.'

'I don't think we can group them as family,' Dr Q said. 'Senthil and his father are family. The other boy has made his own life, as had the dead man.'

'Why did Shaktivel think Senthil had murdered his father? Because the neighbour said so. Why did the neighbour think the murdered man was Subbu Bhagavathar?' Savio repeated Lalli's question to Shaktivel.

'Because they looked alike,' I said. 'The body was prone on the floor. They were dressed alike—'

'Why?' Lalli asked.

'Oh! ' Savio got up abruptly. 'I should have seen that hours ago. I'd better run, then.' And picking up the laptop, he left without another word.

Dr Q looked as mystified as me. Lalli threw her hands up. 'Go figure!'

'Not tonight. Tell us, Lalli,' Dr Q commanded.

'Oh, all right! Take two brothers. One wears the traditional veshti at home and at work. The other dresses for the street in trousers, though he probably relaxes at home in a veshti. So, first inference: as the dead man's wearing a veshti, it must be Subbu Bhagavathar. The neighbours usually observe only the comings and goings of Narayanan, so their mental image of him wears pants. But that day, Narayanan had chosen to arrive in a veshti. So—'

'—so he was mistaken for Subbu,' I finished breathlessly.

'Exactly. So the neighbour observed "Subbu" arrive at eleven—but it was actually Narayanan they saw. Where was Subbu?'

'He had left already—'

'Senthil had left too. Had they left the house unlocked? Or did Narayanan have a key? No to both questions, I'll bet. Narayanan went in because someone was at home. We know where Senthil was between ten and a quarter to twelve. Where was Subbu? Probably at home.'

'If he left after Narayanan arrived, why didn't he say so?' I asked.

'Good question. Senthil arrived around noon—it takes ten minutes to walk home from the temple. He was dressed in his usual dark pants and white shirt. When he was discovered after the murder, he was dressed in blood-soaked veshti and banian. Where are his pants? Where's his white shirt?'

'Folded neatly on the clothesline, I'm sure.'

'There was nothing on that clothesline in the crime scene photos.'

'In the cupboard, then.'

'Well, Savio will tell us soon enough. But here's the puzzle. Why did Senthil change his clothes?'

I was in an unfamiliar room. It was scrubbed clean, unnaturally clean, as if it had been cleared for some ritual.

I smelt disinfectant.

The walls had been washed, they gleamed with wetness. I touched a wet patch, and my finger acquired a pale tinge of red.

I realized I was at the crime scene.

But the crime had been washed away, hadn't it?

What was the stage set for, then?

A shadow fell on the floor, a trellis fanned out.

A bird. A man.

Va, velava, vadivelava, mayil meethu va, the *thillana* invited, but the shadow moved away. I heard Senthil's voice cry out—

'Sita.'

Lalli's hand on my cheek woke me. There was no shadow on the floor, no peacock refusing to dance. The walls were not wet with blood. I was home, in my bed.

'You cried out. Nightmare?'

'No.' I struggled to sit up. 'What time is it?'

'About three a.m.'

'Haven't you slept at all?'

'No. Shall I get you a glass of water?'

'No, I can't go back to sleep. I was dreaming about Ambarnath. Lalli, how do you explain the piercing? That terrible spear going right across the Mayil Azhagan's face?'

'If you're asking for a label, try conversion hysteria. But it's more than that, Sita. It's the preparation—both physical and mental—that induces a different plane of reality. In any state of deprivation, one experiences revelation. Ever wondered why revelations occur on mountains?'

'Low oxygen levels?'

'Probably. But who knows what's real and what's not?'

'Everything is maya?'

'Mortification is the other side of ecstasy, an anthropological truism. But what affected you so deeply? Were you awed? Fascinated? Horrified? Disgusted? Plain scared?'

'A little of all that, but there was this one moment when everything exploded. It didn't explode then, not on that day, but it seems to now, and I can't explain it.'

'Tell me about it.'

'I told you I was watching the Mayil Azhagan and someone was chanting *Kanda Shashti Kavacham*, when a woman fell down with fits. It felt as though the woman's cry had frozen time.'

I had spoken breathlessly, the words tumbling out without thought. There was no question of sleep now. We were both wide awake.

Lalli made coffee and cut some gingerbread.

'And?'

'And yesterday, just before his EEG, I heard Senthil chanting the *kavacham* and realized it was his voice I'd heard at Ambarnath.'

'Ah. That explains the scars on his cheeks. He's been there before.'

'Yes, it explains everything.'

'Sita, you said that to me yesterday too. What does it explain exactly?'

'I don't know,' I admitted miserably. 'I just feel it does.'

'I'm sorry, Sita! The trip was quite an ordeal, and then you had me to look after.'

I had returned home to find Lalli delirious with high fever. I had put the entire experience out of my mind.

'Doesn't make any sense, does it?' I shrugged.

'Not yet, but it will.'

'Shukla had a point when he pointed out you sang *Sri Saraswathi* and *Siddhi Vinayakam* differently. You sang them as if you were teaching a child.'

'Yes!'

'Why? By the way, Ramachandran seemed to know the answer.'

'He should. So should you, since the only intelligent appraisal of the case so far has been yours.'

I awarded myself a second slice of gingerbread, and waited for her to elaborate.

'Why don't you apply your celebrated brain a bit here?' Lalli challenged.

Darn, I couldn't even remember what was so intelligent about my view of the case—

'Oh, the family fell apart when the mother died. The kids were seven. If, say, they started their musical education at three. Would they, that early?'

'In a Bhagavathar's family, definitely. Music's a way of life.'

'So by three or four, the boys would have learnt *Shyamale meenakshi*. By seven, they would have been learning simple *keertanais*. Too early for Dikshitar, surely, Lalli, these are difficult songs.'

'But these two—*Sri Saraswathi* and *Siddhi Vinayakam* are simpler. A teacher would pick these for beginners. And these were talented children.'

'So they began learning—but why do they affect Senthil so badly?'

'Not just Senthil. Guru was deeply disturbed by *Shyamale meenakshi*. The boys aren't just affected by these songs, they're menaced by them.'

'Menaced by Dikshitar *kritis*! It sounds completely crazy.'

'Not all *kritis*. They only know the simple ones. Senthil didn't recognize the other two I sang.'

'But he's not really a musician, is he? He's more into Upanyasam, Thevaram, that sort of thing.'

'That's what his father's taught him. But Senthil is primarily a musician. He won't react with dread to music unless it's associated with pain. I remember Ramachandran saying Senthil didn't want his father to find out this particular song had brought on his fits.'

'So you think Subbu Bhagavathar put a blanket ban on Dikshitar?'

'It's more than a ban. The boys are terrorized by these songs. I must meet this Subbu again today.'

'Perhaps the boys associate these songs with their mother. Perhaps she taught them, not Subbu. And after her death Subbu found it too disturbing to hear these songs, so he banned them.'

'Nice. Let's ask Subbu. Get dressed. Sita, let's take a drive to the crime scene.'

'Lalli, it's four in the morning.'

'Only? I don't know why I feel so compelled. Seven okay for you?'

I nodded, but she had already left the kitchen.

Lalli cancelled the trip after a conversation with Savio. Subbu Bhagavathar had apparently made an early call on Senthil, waking up the constable on guard at six o'clock, saying it was the customary hour for prayers. The nurses protested that Senthil was asleep—but unfortunately he wasn't. Father and son were together for about half an hour, after which Subbu left.

Savio was planning to visit Subbu anyway, so Lalli said there was no point our going, too. She called the ward and spoke to the constable, asking him to inform her the moment Senthil woke up.

'His brother's here, asleep in the corridor, I can wake him if you like,' the constable offered.

'Oh, did the father meet him?' Lalli asked.

'No. He did his puja paat and straight went away.'

'Let me know if the father returns,' Lalli said, and rang off.

She was very nervous all morning.

We heard from Savio around eleven. Subbu was lodged on the temple precincts as his house was sealed off. He was neither sympathetic nor hopeful about Senthil. When Savio mentioned Senthil might need surgery, Subbu flatly refused consent, forgetting he had very recently expected the police to take responsibility for Senthil's treatment. Nothing more was to be had from him.

We heard from the constable late that afternoon. Senthil was still asleep. Savio was in Vashi, on a forgery case. Shukla was not contactable.

Lalli grabbed the car keys. 'Hurry, Sita.'

'Surely, it will be quicker to talk to the nurse or resident—'

'Hurry.'

She slid behind the wheel and floored the accelerator the moment we'd left our lane. It was raining heavily and Lalli was a menace to the madly honking drivers around us as she threaded rapidly past them. From the stern set of her mouth I didn't expect conversation.

I had trouble keeping up with Lalli as she darted into the hospital.

As usual, there was a queue at the elevators, and she took the stairs. Senthil was on the fifth floor, and I was terrified at the consequences this burst of speed might have on Lalli in her present weakened state. I caught up with her as she reached the fourth floor, breathing hard and willing herself on by sheer will.

She braced herself against the wall and gave herself time to recover. Her eyes lost their haunted look. I'd seen her do this before. From now on she would be completely relaxed and at ease.

We strolled up to the constable.

'Still asleep,' he grinned.

Lalli went to the nursing station. 'Patient is sleeping peacefully,' the nurse said blithely. 'Doctor said not to disturb.'

'What sedative is he getting?'

Lalli held out her hand for the chart. No sedation had been ordered. He was on a saline drip for maintenance—nothing more.

A tall man in a white coat approached with a supercilious look.

'Doctor will answer all your questions,' the nurse said in relief.

'What's the problem?'

'That's what I'm here to find out,' Lalli said coldly. 'When did you last examine this patient, Doctor?'

'And you are?'

'Police,' lied Lalli.

'It's a complicated case, madam, but everything's under control.'

'Come with me,' Lalli swept into Senthil's cubicle.

Senthil seemed deeply asleep.

'Wake him up.'

'Eh?'

'Rouse him.'

'He's not ready for questioning now.'

'I don't want to question him. Wake him up.'

When the doctor merely shrugged and glowered silently, Lalli called out Senthil's name.

No response.

A touch on his shoulder didn't wake him.

Lalli pinched his arm—rather cruelly. He didn't flinch in the least.

By now the resident, alarmed, had a torch at the ready. Senthil's pupils reacted sluggishly to light.

'He's in a stupor—likely a metabolic coma,' Lalli said.

'Can't be, he isn't diabetic,' the resident frowned.

'Only one way to find out. Get moving, or do you want me to kick ass?'

He moved.

We retreated to the corridor to let him do his job. The place bustled with nurses now jolted out of inertia.

'Nobody gets near him except hospital staff,' Lalli warned the constable. 'No family, no visitors.'

As if on cue, Guru appeared. 'What's happening? Is something wrong?'

'Yes. When did you last see your brother?'

'Last night. When I came around at eight this morning he was sleeping. The havaldar told me my father was here at six. I was asleep, didn't see him either.'

'Right. There's something very wrong with Senthil now. Let the doctors do their job. Stay here if you can.'

'Of course.'

We hurried away. I looked over my shoulder to see Guru stare after us, bereft.

I didn't ask why we were going the mortuary. Dr Q was just about to start on his autopsies when we arrived. 'What exactly do you suspect, Lalli?' he asked.

'I have no idea. I only know the boy will die.'

'Lalli!' I was drawn to protest.

'Oh yes, he will—and I don't know why. I suspect we'll never know, despite all the tests they'll be running on him now.'

'Science seems to have deserted you this morning,' Dr Q said dryly.

'Has it, Dr Q? Yesterday we saw that seizures may be psychogenic, or may have been caused by the so-called tumour in the temporal lobe. Today we see coma. Metabolic? Brain herniation? Toxic encephalopathy? Who knows! But also, the over-excited brain pressured by event. The sudden surge of memory may behave in ways we can't predict.

The boy has had as much as any human being can bear.'

'Not to mention murder,' Dr Q reminded her.

'Ah, that murder. Senthil murdered nobody, Dr Q. He doesn't have it in him to be cruel. He's terrified of cruelty. He would be out free now if Shukla and Shaktivel had done their jobs. Unfortunately, Savio can't take over. I'll have to do this myself. I'm getting a little old for the regular beat.'

'I first heard you say that thirty years ago. I hear that at least once a year,' Dr Q retorted. 'What about Senthil's condition now? He may regain consciousness only to drift back into stupor. Perhaps Sita should stay. Do you want to question him in a lucid interval?'

'He's unlikely to talk to me.'

'What about Ramachandran? He's coming here in half an hour, I promised to show him a few curios.'

'You've made a friend, Dr Q.'

In answer he extracted a dog-eared volume from his execrable bag and dropped it back quickly before I could catch sight of the title.

'I'm not happy about foisting this on Ramachandran,' Lalli said thoughtfully.

'Oh, he won't think it an imposition, Lalli. He's deeply affected by the boy's plight.'

'Exactly what worries me. Still, he's our best chance. I'll leave it to you to ask him then, Dr Q.

No, Sita, not you. He finds it difficult to say no to you. I'm taking the car, Sita. I'd better hurry. I can't afford to let Senthil down—I've done that once already, God help me!'

And she was gone.

'What did she mean by that?' I exclaimed. 'Should I go after her, Dr Q? She's not herself—'

'No, sit.' Dr Q's hand on my arm compelled me into a chair. 'Take my advice. I've spent a lifetime learning when to leave Lalli alone. You know it's not only this case that's troubling her.'

'But she said she's let Senthil down once already. What could she possibly mean?'

Ramachandran arrived just then. I excused myself hurriedly and stepped out to call Savio. He heard me out worriedly.

'I'm stuck in Vashi, Sita. I'll have a word with Rajesh immediately. You go on ahead to the ward, ask Ramachandran to join you later, just be around.'

'Okay. What should I do if Subbu Bhagavathar turns up to see his son?'

'Call Shukla.'

'Oh hell.'

'Yeah. Got to be faced.'

'He won't stop us from being with Senthil, will he?'

'Let me know if he tries.' That was unusually grim for Savio.

I realized how ignorant I was of the web of

intrigue within the force. Shukla's comment about brain fingerprinting Senthil was not directed at Lalli, but at Savio. Lalli had taken this case on herself to clear that slur. All of us knew that Savio's days in the force were numbered. He just wasn't ready to quit, not just yet.

I returned to Dr Q's office.

'I've called Ponni and told her I'll be here indefinitely,' Ramachandran said. 'Shall we go to Senthil right away?'

'No. He'll probably be whisked around for EEG and imaging and that sort of thing. I'll go and see what's happening and let you know when he's back in the room.'

I hurried to the ward.

The nurse told me the ICU was full, so they were setting up monitors in Senthil's old room. That was a relief. I couldn't imagine Ramachandran being able to have a conversation with Senthil in the ICU.

'Is he going to die?' Guru's voice was calm. He looked like a tightly coiled spring. His eyes had the keenness of a honed knife. The violin could have been a body part, so closely was it moulded against him, and so ligneous was the arm that sheltered it.

'It doesn't look good, Guru. They don't know why he's in a coma.'

'But they can find out, right?'

'They're trying.'

'Where's the other lady—Lalli?'

'Out on the case.'

'So you're police too?'

'No.'

'Oh. Senthil thinks you are.'

'He told you that?'

'Yeah. We talked a lot last night. I wanted to tell Lalli some stuff. What about Inspector Savio?'

'He isn't here today. Inspector Shukla will be here.'

'No, thanks. What about you? Can I talk to you?'

'Sure.'

He waved me towards an alcove. He had made himself comfortable here—backpack, couple of bananas, a packet of biscuits, bottle of water. He grinned. 'Welcome to my life. Banana?'

'Not just now, thanks.' I sat down next to him, back to the wall.

'Never thought he'd talk to me, you know,' Guru said slowly. 'As a stranger maybe, but not like that.'

'Like your brother?'

'Like we haven't been apart for a day. And not as if he asked me about my life or told me about his, you understand. He talked as if we had been together all these years, as though he'd been talking with me every day.'

'He remembers you, then.'

'No. He said, "I can't even remember a time when I had a brother, and now here you are, and I'm in jail, and what can we do about it?" Which is exactly how I felt too. And then he told me this thing: "Ask Police Amma to find my shirt and pants." I tried explaining that he had to stay in hospital clothes, but he insisted that I ask Lalli—or you. Or else, Ramachandran Uncle.'

'I'll convey that to Lalli,' I said. 'So have you been playing for him?'

'Yes, but not the old tunes. I'm too scared of those.'

'What other old tunes do you remember?'

'Want to hear one?'

'Not if it makes you feel bad.'

'Makes me feel terrible, actually. I suppose it brings up painful memories, but I can't say I really remember anything.'

'Later, then.' The poor kid had enough on his plate as it was.

'Do you think Senthil murdered Chittappa?' Guru asked abruptly.

'Do you?' I shot back.

'No.'

'You're very sure.'

'I know Senthil.'

'Actually—you don't.'

'He loved Chittappa. He didn't see him as a loser.'

'Did you?'

'He was—sad. But I prefer him to my father. I don't like my dad. I'm not going back there if Senthil dies.'

'What if he doesn't?'

'We'll see, then.'

'No stroke, no brain edema, no status epilepticus,' Rajesh intoned, 'which means we have no idea what this is.'

'Not metabolic?' I quoted Lalli without any clear idea of what it meant.

'N—no.'

Senthil was back in his room. He looked peacefully asleep. The nurse hooked him to the monitor, adjusted the drip, and assured me he was fine. I didn't ask how she could tell. I called Ramachandran.

I touched Senthil's hand and called his name softly. There was an answering whimper.

I told the nurse to let Dr Rajesh Shah know that the patient was beginning to respond, and returned to my post at his bedside.

Senthil's room led to a small balcony. I opened that door and placed a stool there for myself.

Ramachandran came in hesitantly. He took up a lot of room.

I indicated that he should talk to Senthil, and retreated to the balcony.

It was restful watching the bi-directional flow of traffic five stories below. It moved at a constant speed, punctuated by pauses at regular intervals. The predictability was anodyne.

The sun had come out, a watery sun, wringing out its beams in the steamy air. A treetop two floors below me exploded with crows, then shook its umbel dry in a sudden gust that seized a tardy crow and sent it reeling off course.

The manic honking in the street had eased up. The rain kept up its breathless chatter.

Ramachandran's low rumble reached me like the buzzing of a distant bee. I peeped in. He was chatting with the sleeping boy. Every now and then he paused as if expecting an answer. Senthil made no response.

'Could you sing something?'

'I don't know what he likes.'

'No, do what you did the other day. Sing what you think he might want now.'

I left him to it.

In a few moments he began an *alapanai* at a very low pitch, very soft, no more than the murmur of the tide. When the *pallavi* took wing, it was an easy glide just skimming over the tide. I held my breath for what must follow—and here it came, vibrating at an impossible height, gliding, cavorting, circling, till it plummeted to its original easy glide, tumbling in effortless glissando.

Raga sudha rasa, panamu chese... Come drink the nectar of music, my soul.

He kept singing the melody, sinking the pitch still further till it lost itself in the pluvial hush.

I restrained myself from looking in, but a few

minutes later, Ramachandran beckoned from the doorway.

Senthil's eyes were open, roving the room. They rested on us for a moment, then passed beyond without any sign of recognition.

'Senthil,' Ramachandran's voice brought back Senthil's gaze. 'Here's some vibhuti.'

Ramachandran took a small package from his pocket and drew a stripe of ash across Senthil's forehead. Senthil shut his eyes with a beatific smile.

'It's the vibhuti you gave me, Senthil,' Ramachandran said.

'I know. Sing, please. Call him.'

'Call whom, Senthil? Guru?'

'Guru guha! Muruga! Arumuga!'

Senthil's eyes were fixed on the distance, straining to focus. Was he looking for Murugan? Arumuga, his six-faced God?

Arumo en aaval, arumuganai neril kaanada arumu... Will my ardour cease without beholding Arumuga?

As Ramachandran sang the aching cry of the devotee for one glimpse of the beloved, Senthil's lips moved soundlessly in accompaniment. Tears spilled down his cheeks. When the song was over, he turned his face and looked at me.

'Tell Police Amma.'

'Tell her what, Senthil?'

'Everything. Everything.' His face changed and grew stern. 'Tell her I remember everything.'

'What is everything, Senthil?' I asked, sinking my voice, for he seemed to respond best to a low tone.

'Everything is Sivam. *Anbe Sivam*.'

'What do you remember, Senthil?'

'Call him again, Mama. He will come dancing if you sing.'

'Yes, I'll call him. As I call him, tell us what you remember.'

'He's calling me, I have to go now.' A sudden agitation seized him. His eyes rolled wildly, searching the room. 'Arumuga, couldn't you save me from him?'

'From whom, Senthil?'

'From whom? From the five-faced one—Ainthumugan! Ainthumugan!'

His agitation increased.

I thought I should call the doctor and moved towards the door.

'Don't go! How will you tell Police Amma if you leave now? Wait, wait he will be here soon—Tell her it was the five-faced one, don't forget.'

'Shall I call Guru?'

'No! Not Guru! He doesn't remember anything. Don't tell him, or the five-faced one will kill him too!'

He raised himself and caught Ramachandran's hand. 'Call him, sing!'

Ramachandran, sweat rolling down his trembling cheeks, shut his eyes and sang the delicate *thillana* in

Shivaranjani I had heard—was it only last evening? And, at almost the same hour, for the light was beginning to fail outside. The filigreed notes sounded even more ethereal in the violet haze of dusk.

Senthil held on to Ramachandran's hand, but his eyes were fixed with growing wonder on the distance. Ramachandran continued to sing with his eyes shut as if the sound was being forced out of his throat by a supreme act of will. He reached the lyrics at last.

Va velava, vadivelava, nee mayil meedu nee va... Kumara, va!

As he repeated the line, Senthil's eyes lost their distance. They came into focus with a flash of recognition.

He gave a glad cry, loud and jubilant. 'Amma!'

And, died.

In the confusion that followed, with doctors and nurses milling around, I coaxed Ramachandran out of the room. He seemed more than just shaken. I took his hand in alarm. It was icy. His lips were turning grey. He doubled up, and collapsed on the floor. I knelt by him, shouting desperately for help. He tried to say something, but no words came. I ran behind the trolley as he was wheeled into the ICU.

The glass doors shut, leaving me to face impossibilities.

What was I going to tell Ponni?

The door opened and a resident stuck out his head.

'You with him? Massive infarct. He's pretty critical... frankly, I don't know if he'll make it. Doing our best.'

I tried Lalli's number, but she'd switched off her phone. I got Dr Q and was somehow coherent enough. I caught sight of Guru.

For a long moment we faced each other in silence.

Then he asked, 'Did my brother say anything before he died?'

I couldn't repeat Senthil's delirium about the six-faced god and the five-faced man.

'What were his last words?'

That I could answer.

'He cried out "Amma!" just before he died.'

Guru nodded. 'I thought so. I remembered her too, at that exact moment. I too saw her face just before he died.'

Dr Q saved me from replying just then. He took charge of the shattered day, explanations, phone calls, reassurances, the lot. Patherphaker and Manda Tai would accompany Ponni to hospital, that was a relief.

There was nothing to do but wait.

'Now that Senthil's dead,' Guru said slowly, 'who will clear his name?'

'I will,' Lalli's quiet voice replied.

I hadn't seen Lalli come in. I had been distracted

by the vision of Shukla and Shaktivel staring at Senthil's body.

Freed of torment, Senthil's face radiated a majestic calm. The open eyes seemed clear and assertive.

Shukla's face changed. He took a step backward, his eyes clouding, his brow contracting. When Shaktivel bent towards the body, Shukla restrained him.

'Call Dr Q!' he ordered.

'What for, sir? Death is from epilepsy. Good much saving of our time and money.'

'Get out!' Shukla snarled. Catching my eye, he turned suddenly savage, sweeping things off the little table next to the bed, pulling off the sensors from Senthil's body, kicking the drip stand away and raising general mayhem.

Arrested development, definitely.

It's a gender thing. Boys of ten or twelve expect the world to read the tantrum as general self-loathing, regret and apology.

Girls cry.

Lalli confronted Shukla as he emerged from Senthil's room.

She held out her hand. 'Come with me, Shukla, let's see this through.'

He took her hand in both his, too disturbed for words.

'Case is closed, madam,' Shaktivel piped up.

'Murderer is dead, time to celebrate.' He had gloat written all over his fat face.

I held my breath.

Lalli, Shukla, Guru—which of them would punch Shaktivel?

My money was on Guru, but Lalli did it. Her fist sprang before I could blink and crashed into Shaktivel's jaw, sending him reeling.

'The case isn't closed. It's just been cracked wide open. Learn to do your job better instead of slandering the dead!' Lalli said coldly.

'Madam, you have assaulted a police officer.' Shaktivel regained his balance and his bluster.

Lalli laughed and swept past him.

'Did you really mean that?' I asked, running to keep pace with her.

'What, the punch?'

'No, that the case is cracked.'

'Certainly! Shaktivel's idiocy has lost us most of the evidence, but we're getting there. Guru's told me about Ramachandran—I brought this on him, Sita!'

She stopped abruptly and faced me, her face a tight knot of misery, mirrored my own.

'It wasn't you,' I assured her lamely. 'It was something Senthil said, or else the trauma of singing to him that brought on Ramachandran's heart attack.'

'Tell me.'

I rapidly recounted Senthil's last hour. 'He was

completely delirious towards the end, all that blather about Arumugam and the five-faced man, Ainthumugam—'

'What did Ramachandran say about it?'

'He couldn't say anything. He tried to, but by then he was in severe pain. It looks bad, Lalli.'

She held out the car keys. 'Do you feel up to driving? Or should I ask Shukla to drop you home?'

'You're staying?' A redundant question.

She put her arm around me. It felt like a band of steel.

Suddenly, it tightened alarmingly.

I hastily freed myself, but she didn't even notice. She was staring straight ahead, eyes dilated. She wasn't looking. She was *listening*.

Guru was at his brother's bedside, playing the violin. The notes welled lugubrious, out of sync, hesitant.

He was playing one of his 'old tunes,' playing it so badly it was barely recognizable as Dikshitar's *Kanjadalayatakshi*.

One look at Lalli told me she had found her lost tune.

Going home was my ultimate act of cowardice. I was relieved I didn't have to face Ponni. I had already abandoned Ramachandran. I had been of no help to Senthil in his last moments. And now, ignoring Lalli's exhaustion and fragility, I had left her to deal with Ponni's reproaches.

The only way I could live through that endless drive home was by letting loose all the music trapped in my head. I sang, tunelessly, despairingly, knowing none of the sounds I produced matched those in my brain, but just the same, the music kept me going.

The empty house folded its wings around me as I crouched empty-hearted in the armchair. Night crept into the house like ink, staining everything with darkness except my watchful and awakened brain. Sometime past midnight, I heard Savio's bike at the gate. He let himself in and switched on the light.

Ignoring me, he went into the kitchen and messed about, returning with a sandwich and some truly vile coffee that he forced down my throat.

'Swallow. You're a threatened species, Forest Owlet.'

I suppose I was, staring in the dark.

I settled into him with relief, not needing to explain.

The day replayed in silence.

I wondered what Senthil's delirious ranting had meant to him.

Ainthumugan—five-faced one—was not recognizable from any myth.

Why did Senthil's brain invent him?

I don't know what made me change gear—but what if Senthil's brain hadn't invented any of that?

'What?'

'I didn't say anything.'

'No, but a thought startled you.'

'What if—'

I took a deep breath and launched into a description of the celebration at Ambarnath, and then of Senthil's last hour.

'What if it was that man Senthil meant, the one being transformed with the peacock kavadi into Murugan?'

'No. That guy had only one head. Senthil saw six.'

'Savio, if the man was transformed into Murugan, then in Senthil's eyes he would have six heads!'

'No, he wouldn't. If it was *that* man Senthil pictured, he would have hailed him in the name appropriate to his vision. Muruga! Kumara! Not as six-faced Arumuga!'

'So what was it?'

'Senthil definitely saw his adored God.'

'But who's the guy with five heads then? There ain't no such myth.'

'Must be. This is one thing he couldn't actually have seen, right? So it's a metaphor. Or, he was raving. One of the two.'

Savio has a way of clearing my thoughts. It felt blissful now to have only two possibilities to consider—metaphor or madness.

Music had invaded my brain since I realized Lalli was in trouble. Its descant of alarm permeated every thought. Dr Q said Ramachandran thought in music.

I wondered what song filled him now as he battled for his life.

'He'll pull through, Sita.' Savio's murmur didn't console me in the least.

It was not Lalli, but I who had endangered Ramachandran by asking him to sing.

'What happens when you put your entire soul, your entire life, into five minutes?'

'In what way?'

'Ramachandran did that when he sang. The emotion was beyond endurance and his heart gave out. Was that what happened?'

'The same way poor Senthil got fits. Let's hope that doesn't happen to Guru too. Sita, I've been thinking of your view of the case. Perhaps, the key is the mother's death—'

'Did I tell you how Senthil cried out "Amma"? Just before he died. And when I told Guru, he said he had seen his mother too, at the same moment. Eerie!'

'Not really. That's just wish fulfillment. I see my mother very often.'

'You do? You've never told me that before.'

'What's to tell? I see her and I know I'm real.'

His words sank in with peculiar significance. Was it true of all of us, then? Was each person's reality defined by the unreal?

I let that one go.

The fear-filled days of July when Lalli's distress

began were the first notes of a *raagam* slowly unfurling its melodic profile. Now it had developed rhythm. It was now defined by events that pointed inexorably to an appointed course. Freewheeling dread had now acquired a code. Restricted as the few syllables of a *taanam* which must compress the entire spectrum of the *raagam*, it was just as meaningless as those palindromic notes *anantam, anandam*. And yet, its elaboration contained the whole story.

Lalli's face told me she had understood it.

How would the *pallavi* unfold? Would it begin with a *padam*, a clear statement of fact—one we should have guessed as *raagam* and *taanam* were building? It would require *layam,* elaboration of each phrase and argument. And then *vinyasam*, where each piece of the puzzle found its appointed slot.

Pallavi

Padam

Ramachandran was still critical—but alive. Lalli brought home the news at seven.

Ponni was less resilient. After her initial shock, she had dissolved into complete helplessness. Throughout, she had refused to call their daughter in Florida.

'I don't want to worry her,' she kept muttering.

Patherphaker had pointed out that Ramachandran might want otherwise, but Ponni was adamant.

Lalli said that Patherphaker wouldn't take the hint until Ponni had said, very bravely, considering the situation, 'We have children enough here, don't we?'

Guru, who had stayed back in the hospital, apparently qualified.

'He's quite dependable, and I'm relieved because I didn't want him going home,' Lalli said.

'Why ever not?' I asked.

Lalli didn't answer that, but she did say if Dr Q had the autopsy done early, she was in no hurry to release Senthil's body.

'I'm going there now,' Savio said, crunching his last triangle of toast. 'Anything else?'

'Yes—but only if I call you.'

I had packed a brunch for Ponni knowing she would refuse to leave that corridor, convinced that her absence even for a minute would tip the tenuous balance of her husband's life.

I was confused by Lalli's appearance. She looked relaxed, almost joyous, fresh in a crisp blue and ivory cotton sari. A delicate perfume, evanescent as coral jasmine, shimmered around her. Gone was the tortured clench of the past few weeks.

I was too relieved to question this change. Above all, I breathed easy that she now realized she never could have committed murder. Needless to say, I hadn't believed her for one moment. It was just some kind of—

'Fantasy? Oh no, no. It's real. As tangible as this.' She knocked the table with her knuckles.

'What are you talking about?'

'Really, Sita? If you wish to hide your thoughts you must cultivate some kind of mask. You were wondering if my murder was just a confused dream, seeing me energized today. Right?'

'I didn't think it showed.'

She laughed and handed me a lavishly buttered piece of hot toast, just ready for a slide of marmalade.

'Not only was the murder real, I've remembered enough to tell you the first part of the story. You'll have to wait till our visitor's been—she'll be here by ten, I hope. Till then, would it be too hard on you to recall last evening? See if you can remember Senthil's exact words.'

'He was raving, Lalli. He ranted as if he was hallucinating.'

'Yes, that's very likely. But what did he see?'

'He saw, or wanted to see, his beloved Murugan. He asked Ramachandran to call him with song. And then, when Ramachandran sang the line *Va, velava, vadivelava,* Senthil's face suddenly became alert, as if he recognized something. He cried out "Amma!" And the next moment it was over.'

'You think he saw his mother, or he saw Murugan?'

'It's strange you should ask that, Lalli. Savio and I argued over this. Remember the peacock kavadi I told you about, at Ambarnath?'

'The Mayil Azhagan you were watching when you heard Senthil's voice?'

'Yes, that guy. Lalli, I had the weirdest feeling it was that man Senthil saw yesterday as he cried out Arumuga! His vision was not of the boy god on his peacock, but of this young man carrying the metal kavadi embedded in his torso. I suppose it's just my imagination—'

'What were his exact words? Can you recall them?'

'I'll never forget them, Lalli! The anguish with

which he cried out: "Arumuga, you couldn't save me from him!" I asked him from whom. And he answered, "From him! From the man with five heads, Ainthumugan! Ainthumugan!"'

'I *see.*'

'Earlier, he asked me to tell you he remembered everything.'

'Poor child, poor child…' Lalli couldn't hold back her tears. 'I failed him once, Sita, so badly. I can't fail him again, not after he's told me everything.'

Senthil hadn't told her anything, as far as as I could gather.

'You said that once before, Lalli. When did you ever fail Senthil?'

Her face resumed its iron mask of sternness as she said, 'When I committed murder.'

Our visitor, who arrived punctually at ten, was a slip of a girl, much older than her appearance suggested. Dressed in a green shalwar kameez, hair plaited neatly, she looked barely eighteen. She carried a white plastic bag clutched close and wrapped in her generous dupatta.

I realized my mistake when she spoke—she was thirty, or more. She had the cluck of a woman kept constantly at work tucking in loose ends, ironing out creases, smoothing wrinkles, reaching for that spoonful of sugar to be sprinkled on every dose of hemlock the world held out.

'You're very like your mother, Shaheen,' Lalli smiled.

'So they tell me. And you're very like—this.' She took out a heavy folder from the bag and flipping swiftly through it, extracted a sheet of paper that she held out to Lalli.

'But—'

It was a long time since I'd seen Lalli so taken aback.

Shaheen dimpled very prettily. 'It's a good likeness, yes?'

Lalli gave me the drawing. It was a bravura sketch, executed in pastels, and as intelligent an appraisal of Lalli as it was a good likeness.

The only thing the artist had got wrong was her hair—the artist had given her a severe, almost metallic chignon.

'And you drew this? I don't remember our ever meeting, Shaheen. From a photograph, then.'

'No, a photograph would have shown your hair as is,' I protested.

Both of them laughed.

'She's right, it's from a photograph—'

'A very old photograph—'

'This one!'

I've seen very few old pictures of my aunt.

This photo, inscribed *For Munira, with love*, showed my aunt very different from what I had imagined. The gallant tilt of chin was the same, but the intelligent eyes were full of pain, the smile ironic. Her hair was hidden under her cap.

The date beneath her signature was 15th October 1995.

'Mummy told me a great deal about you. So I imagined this is what you must look like now. I made the sketch last evening after you called. Please keep it.'

'Of course, I will. So, what do you do with this superb talent of yours, Shaheen?'

'I look after my husband, two kids, a bed-ridden father-in-law.'

'And?'

'I want a job. Here's the picture you asked for.'

Lalli uttered a small cry when she saw the drawing. Before she could show it to me, Shaheen handed her another. 'And here is the picture you will now ask for.'

The first picture showed a woman in her forties. There was a large crimson kumkuma pottu on her forehead. Her large eyes were bitter with rage, yet the features had a preternatural calm. The mouth, beautiful in its curve, had an impassivity that spoke of iron control, not arrogance. She was devoid of the ornaments I expected—no earrings, and the slender neck was bare. It was a lovely face, distorted by something beyond rage. Grief. This was a woman beset by grief.

The second portrait drew a cry from me.

It was the same face, aged, as Lalli's had been aged. I knew this face—knew was too strong a word—I had seen it somewhere before.

The artist—this was Shaheen's work—had softened the glare in the eyes, but they were still distressed. The face was lined, the features rendered more distinct by the thinned cheeks, the mouth more relaxed. The face was hauntingly familiar, but I couldn't place it.

'Of course, you have computers doing all this,' Shaheen said, almost pleadingly. 'My skill has been overtaken by technology. I can't adapt to computers, I've tried and given up.'

'Yes, we do have computers doing this sort of thing, Shaheen, but I won't agree when you say your skills have been superseded by them. I'll call you in a day or two. Meanwhile, I'm going to keep all three drawings.'

'And may I keep the photograph?' I asked.

Shaheen looked as if she'd willingly gift Lalli the whole folder, but she nodded brightly to me, thanked Lalli and left.

I picked up the photograph. 'It was a bad time, Lalli?'

Her face closed like a fist. But the next instant, something made her relent. She leaned forward, hands clenched, intent.

'If only I had conceded to myself, Sita, how bad it was, how I had imploded with pain, if only I had admitted it, instead of trying to survive. I survived, but at what cost? My dishonesty, my denial, my cowardice—they added up to murder.'

Silence quivered raw and burning in the flayed air. Then her face cleared and she touched my cheek gently.

'Don't grieve, Sita. It's over and done with now.'

Not for me. I had just woken up to the truth that my aunt's life had been shaped as much by pain as by adventure. Which of these compelled her relentless pursuit of truth?

She picked up Munira's sketch and looked at it for a long while in silence.

'Munira had a tough life. She would have wished an easier one on her daughter,' she sighed.

She turned the drawing over and showed me the date: 5th October 1995.

Kanniya Kumari, 5 October 1995

Lalli reached Kanyakumari late in the afternoon. She was here to make an arrest. Her presence was a mere formality, necessary to complete the paperwork, and to apply closure to a manhunt that had taken up four years of her life.

The news that she had run her quarry down to ground at last, at the very tip of the subcontinent, had come at a time of great personal conflict.

There was none of the elation she had thought she would feel. A sheaf of papers to sign, the magic words to be pronounced, and it was back to Bombay on the night train.

Business quickly over, Lalli hurried to the ocean.

There was nothing else she had thought of since she had jumped off that jeep two hours ago. Unseen all this while, as she was hurried from one concrete block to another, the ocean had dominated her thoughts, everything was upheld by the loft of its roar.

'Ocean's engine is always running,' Inspector Jacob shouted. 'All our energies have to be pitched above it.'

It was an insane ambition.

It was a still afternoon, but Lalli could imagine what the wind could do, roll up the town into a tight huddle, helpless against the whiplash.

The smell of the ocean, clean, briny, seared the airway down to the very edges of her lungs.

'How can you bear to live indoors?' she asked Jacob.

'Tell us when you're coming next, we'll get you a tent on the beach,' he grinned. 'If there's any beach left by then.'

'Why, where's it going? Coastal erosion?'

'That's a term I don't understand. Lalli, our Kanniya Kumari floats on a huge reef of coral. For three thousand years it's endured us, now with Vivekanandas and Gandhis to be worshipped, we've started pouring concrete by the ton. Look at the plans on paper.'

'What plans?'

'Giant statue of Thiruvalluvar coming up in a year or two. Tallest statue in Asia. Guardian of the subcontinent—fools up north haven't even heard his name and fools here haven't read the Kural. Our guardian's stood here for millennia, we don't need one more. Bhagavathi or Mary, call her what you want, but she's all the guardian we need.'

'What's that legend about the diamond in her nose-ring that wrecked ships out at sea?'

'The temple keeps the eastern door shut because of that legend. Of course the ships that get wrecked are always pirates and enemies. The good guys are guided into port.'

'Of course.'

'Including the Portuguese who built a church in thanksgiving for letting them rape the land. But I think you'd like to look around on your own, eh? Dinner at my place? First class meen kozhambu, that I can promise you.'

'It'll have to be next time, Jacob. My train's at eight.'

'Right then, I'll have the jeep waiting for you at half past seven.'

He drove off with a cheery wave, and Lalli felt her first exhilarating moment of utter freedom.

Not just the day, but her entire life seemed to lift off her like a husk, leaving her this iridescent moment.

She ran towards the strand.

Most of the beach had already been walled off. It was breached at one point which was now plugged with a colourful procession of Gujarati women spilling out from a tourist bus. It would take a while before she could squeeze her way through.

Lalli regretted having changed into a sari. It would have been easier to let herself down over the rocks in uniform, but that was out of the question now. She was to be cheated of the spectacular sunset too. It was overcast. The horizon, a brilliant streak of violet, hinged the sullen dichotomy of grey. For now, the ocean sulked, turning its broad back on a teasing wind that ruffled its frothy curls. But it would erupt soon.

'By the time the light fades, you'll hear the water roar,' a voice said at Lalli's elbow. A tiny woman of about seventy smiled up at her. 'You've come here to see the ocean, haven't you. But it's out of temper today.'

'You know it well, I think.'

'Father, mother, husband, child, it's everything to me.'

Arms akimbo she stared at its immensity with an exasperated sigh.

'You don't think this calm will last?'

'Calm? This is not calm, it's just getting ready. But these days it doesn't know its own mind.'

'Why do you say that?'

'Look around, and you'll know.' She pointed to the concrete wall and its narrow ingress. 'Poisons the water. Creatures die. I hardly get any good shells anymore.'

'You sell shells?'

She smiled broadly and said carefully, in English, 'She sells seashells by the seashore. Come, I'll show you.'

Her stall was in a cove, a little further away. It had a banner with the tongue-twister painted in red letters.

'My grand-daughter learned that in school, so I thought why not? It's a nice enough name for my stall.'

Her wares ranged from the humble cowrie to grandiose corals.

'It will last maybe a year or more, then we'll all lose our place here,' she said. 'It's all politics now.

They've taken over the temple, what more can I say?'

'Taken over?'

'New people everywhere. They don't know the language, they don't know the customs. How can they know our Bhagavathi?'

Lalli paid up for her modest purchase and was about to leave when the woman said, 'Here, take this, it's free.' She held out a delicate conch ribbed with pink and brown, translucent, perfect in its whorl. It twinkled on her calloused palm like a jewel.

'Keep it.' She turned away, dismissing Lalli's thanks.

Heartened by the impulsive gift, Lalli hurried, clutching her treasure, without quite knowing where she was headed.

She was led by her nose. The briny sting of the ocean was now tinged with warmer scents. A twist of the subtle and the keen, of sweetness and savagery, permeated the air now, bringing with it a rush of appetite. It was the eternal lure—spice.

The spice market, dark, dry, under a ribbed canopy raised on shiny wooden rafters, held its bubble of fragrance tight against the intrusion of the ocean. It was almost as if its enclave had been shaped to contain the force of human endeavour pitted against the elements.

Within, it was not dark, but muted. Lalli's eyes adjusted to a very restricted palette of grey and brown. The colours on display in no-nonsense bins went from the pallid jade of cardamom, to intense black buckyballs of pepper. The scents that had made so voluptuous an accord minutes ago had now retreated, distinct and inviolate. Silky tendrils of odour pulsed above each bin, spinning a protective cocoon for its treasure. Everything was hushed in here

Lalli bought with mad abandon: cinnamon, cloves, nutmeg, mace, three sorts of cardamom, pepper, more pepper…

It was long past six.

She must hurry if she wanted to see the temple. Here it was, just beyond the market.

'Could you hold on to this for me?' she asked the shopkeeper. 'I'll collect it on my way out.'

'Sure. You'll be back before the Kutcheri?'

'Kutcheri? There's a concert tonight? Here?'

'At the navaratri mandapam. Begins at eight. It's worth hearing.'

'Wish I could stay, but my train leaves at eight.'

'Bombay?'

'Yes.'

'Take your time at the temple. Your things are safe here.'

Lalli still had the conch in her grasp—too late to walk back to the shop and pop it into her bag now.

Like other old temples, Kanniya Kumari's too was peripatetic, built over the centuries by this ruler or that, but the shrine was probably as old as human habitation.

The cult of the virgin goddess was universal, only the legends differed.

Balambika, the Kanni of Kumari Kandam, now guarded the coast, but her ancient purpose was to destroy the demon Banasura. She was distracted from her purpose by falling in love with Shiva, so irresistible in his wild generosity. And he? How could he not adore this luminous slip of a girl, so gallant with mischief? So they were to be married.

But happy endings have no place in human memory. The meddling gods reminded Narada of the prophecy—the dreaded demon could only be killed by a virgin. It was up to Narada to stop the wedding.

The auspicious hour was Brahmamuhurta, one hour and thirty-six minutes before sunrise, and the bridegroom's party at Suchindram, a few miles away, was all set for the ceremonial trek to Kanniya Kumari—when a cock crowed.

It was Narada, of course, up to his wily tricks.

Shiva—confused and befuddled as usual—decided he had missed the bus this time.

It was dawn already, the auspicious hour was long past, might as well get an hour's shut-eye before he caught up with the cosmos.

Bala, anguished, tore off her jewels and flung them into the ocean. She rushed to the kitchen and hurled the delicacies of the wedding feast every which way on the strand.

And there they've stayed, vitrified as particles of multicoloured sand.

Balambika grew stern and isolated. Banasura, intrigued by her icy reserve, began to badger her. He stalked and waylaid her. Humbly, he wooed her. And rejected, he retaliated with hate.

Outraged, Balambika killed Banasura.

And having got a reputation for that sort of thing, Bala took on assorted demons who dared to menace her devotees. For the rest, she remained chaste and protective, guarding the ocean and the land.

The temple was dedicated not to that ascetic maiden, but to the child Balambika, still joyous and full of mischief, unprepared for the panic of puberty and a despairing love.

The carvings on the pillars and friezes were charming, showing little girls at play, antic animals and birds and ornamental foliage. There were no erotic images, no seductive apsaras, amorous couples, ithyphallic sages, no heroes with orgiastic groupies.

As she circumambulated the pradakshina, Lalli was enchanted by the freedom of the space. The sacred had been tutored to respect human priorities. In a country so vitiated by its hatred of daughters, this temple was a sanctuary. Lalli felt, in that despairing part of her soul, a tiny plumule of hope.

She caught sight of the temple elephants in the

verandah beyond. Leaving the pradakshina, she approached them.

The first one appraised her with a mildly ironic eye. There was something humourous about him. He was young and strong, and Lalli regretted his shackles. As if to reassure her, he swung his trunk playfully and held it out to her. She patted it and moved to his partner, a leaner beast, restlessly shifting on her gargantuan feet. As she moved to the other side of this elephant, she felt a gentle pressure on her shoulder, drawing her away.

'Pardon me, but let me explain.'

It was an elderly pujari with folded hands, asking her pardon for his touch.

'She's an old elephant, almost as old as me! Eighty-two. Blind in the left eye. She strikes out madly at anyone who approaches her on the left. I had to pull you away!'

'Thank you for your kindness—'

'Not everyone's used to elephants. Kalyani and I have grown old together, we know each other's ways,' he smiled. 'Have you had darshanam? Not yet? I won't hold you up.'

'There have been many changes here of late?'

'Too many. But who am I to complain? Change is the order of existence.'

'Still, it's hard to face. This is an ancient temple.'

'This is Her home. We are all guests for a lifetime. She is eternal. We keep to the old ways—but for how long? Now there are pujaris from other places. From the north. My people have been born to this duty probably for a thousand years. We know no other life, just as the fisherfolk here know no other life. What will our sons and daughters do? Should my son worry about his son's future or concentrate on serving Bhagavathi? We are freed from the burden of such worries when our families are consecrated to Her—but no longer. Here, child, take this.'

He placed a pinch of kumkumam on her palm. His blessing worried Lalli. He departed from the usual formula and said instead, 'Be vigilant, be fearless.'

The eastern door was shut, nonetheless, the ocean's roar filled the sanctum as Lalli approached the garbha graham. This evening, the womblike space was brightly lit. The multi-tiered lamps suffused a golden radiance. The crowd of devotees had stopped shuffling and murmuring. The silence of expectation enveloped the worshippers.

Lalli was unprepared for the delight she felt at her first sight of Balambika. A chandanakaapu, a mask of sandalwood paste, applied to throw the granite features in relief, had transformed the sacred and unapproachable into the human and immediate.

Here was a lovely girl, her eyes dancing with mischief, delighted with her rose pattu pavadai and her jewels, excited as any thirteen-year-old over the fragrant garlands of jasmine and roses, heady with tulsi, thyme, patchouli and spikenard. The air sang with sandalwood and camphor. The hushed throng, wonderstruck, gazed mesmerized.

Lalli remembered the elderly man's words as she glimpsed the officiating pujari, preparing for the arati. A middle-aged man. From the colour of his skin and the cut of his hair, not from these parts. His sonorous recitation of the sloka was hurried and unmusical—perhaps that was what attracted Lalli's attention to his discomfort.

The man's eyes were elsewhere.

His broad forehead had a sheen of sweat.

The pulse at his temple grew faster as Lalli watched. His fat jowls flushed, his lips glistened.

He was a man unbearably aroused.

For an instant his roving eyes met Lalli's, startling her.

The limpid brown irises burned like lamps, pupils flying open as they focused on her with a predator's glare.

Lalli looked away hastily, then, angry at herself, glared back till, with something like a smile, his eyes slid off her, prowling again.

Lalli forced herself to calm down, but her outrage was not at being the target for the man's concupiscent stare.

A moment ago, she had surprised his discomfort. She guessed he had been more than embarrassed then. Appalled, probably, at the rush of desire that had ambushed him so inappropriately.

A simple biological reflex, easily quelled. But the very next instant he had given it free rein. He was no longer moved by desire, he was armed by it.

Having swept the crowd with his lascivious stare, once, twice, a third time with maddened intent, his eyes steadied. With slow deliberation he turned that gaze on the goddess.

She could no longer watch his face, but Lalli knew it hadn't changed. It was still slavering, brutish, predatory.

The radiant young girl smiled trustingly at him, glowing in her aura of lamplight and incense. Any minute she would toss away her garlands and rush off twinkle-toed on some new mad caprice.

The pujari strained, neck craned, his vulpine crouch spring-loaded, raking the laughing teenager with his eyes.

Somebody cried out—a sound between gasp and whimper.

There was a confused murmur as people turned, roused from their enchantment. The pujari stepped back in confusion, letting his tray of flowers slide to the floor. Bells rang out in glad relief. Two acolytes approached with pyramids of flaming camphor, making way for an older priest to commence the ritual within the garbha griha, and the crowd returned with a sigh to its earnest contemplation.

Lalli, though, had caught sight of the woman who cried out the moment the pujari had turned to face the deity.

She was of Lalli's age, hair knotted carelessly, straggling ends stuck to her straining neck that glistened with sweat. It was her eyes that Lalli noticed first. They were black pits of venom, studding a face that seemed frozen in a grimace of revulsion. The bold kumukuma pottu on her forehead was bisected by her frown.

The target of her contempt had now moved off, leaving the ritual to the other celebrants.

Lalli was surprised to find herself still trembling with outrage.

The pujari's folly had erased the very purpose of the temple. And how illogical that was. The sacred and the profane were both human ideas, and what could be more human than desire?

No, it was not illogical at all. The man's offence was not his unexpected lust, or even his flagrantly predatory leer at the congregation. It was his disregard for his office. His contempt for the innocence that shone at him from the garbha griha, this sanctuary of girlhood. *That* was what he mocked.

Confused and disturbed, Lalli pushed her way out through the crowd.

She looked around, but the woman she had noticed was nowhere to be seen.

Lalli almost forgot her purchase—the spice vendor

called out to her, cutting short his pleasantries as he took in her state. She grabbed her bag and hurried away.

Night had fallen now, the darkness made more ghastly by the greenish flare of street lamps.

Something was wrong—Lalli realized she had dropped the conch she had been clutching all evening. She remembered feeling its edge against her palm when she picked up her bag. It must have fallen just a few yards away.

Lalli retraced her steps. There was something on the pavement, just under the streetlamp—yes, that must be it.

Just then a woman emerged from the shop next to the spice market. It was a shop that sold household items, utensils, cutlery, mops, incongruous in this line of souvenir shops, as though a passing tourist might urgently need a pair of kitchen tongs or a mop.

The figure in the street lamp's spotlight looked vaguely familiar. It was the woman who had cried out. She clutched her purchase, something long and slender, wrapped in newspaper.

Lalli watched helplessly as the woman bent to pick up the conch. She wiped it carefully with her sari and looked up. She looked straight at Lalli and through her.

Her face, calm, intent, determined, resembled someone Lalli knew, but she couldn't place the resemblance. She considered calling out to claim her conch, then, thinking better of it, walked away.

Back in the whirl of mayhem in Bombay, Lalli had almost forgotten the incident when Jacob called a week later.

'Too bad you put off dinner with us that night, Lalli, or you would have stayed back in Kumari for a day or two.'

'Why?'

'There was a terrible incident here, at the temple.'

Lalli's senses flared on alert.

'A pujari was murdered. Stabbed as he was walking home. One of the new fellows we know nothing about. No leads, not one.'

'A young man?'

'No. Fifty-ish. Why do you ask?'

'There were these two young pujaris and a very old man at the arati that evening, so—' Lalli lied, trying to quiet a rush of palpitations.

'Ah. Missed you. You would have thought outside the box, come up with something.'

Lalli convinced herself it was all her imagination. Her agitation and revulsion towards the poor man could hardly have resulted in his murder. The woman she had noticed had shared her outrage. Her only crime had been to appropriate Lalli's conch.

Nonetheless, that evening, Lalli paid Munira a visit and asked her to sketch a face she recalled feature by feature. Munira's sketch was as faithful as a photograph.

Again, it reminded Lalli disquietingly of someone else.

Jacob didn't call again, and the incident passed out of Lalli's memory.

'*That's* your murder?' I asked incredulously. 'You didn't kill anybody, Lalli!'

'I did, Sita. You see, in some hidden layer of my mind *I knew before the fact*.'

'Anybody would have been distressed by that incident. That woman was, too. You have nothing to tell you that she killed the priest. Or even whether it was the same priest.'

'That was the only point I ascertained. It was the same man. '

'So what? There's nothing to tell you the woman had anything to do with his murder.'

'I saw her buying the weapon, Sita, and you say that! The package she had with her—it was a knife. A large kitchen knife. All I had to do was to give Jacob that detail.'

'Why didn't you?'

'Exactly. I knew you'd agree, eventually.'

'I haven't agreed to anything. You didn't tell Jacob, yes, that was culpable. But all you had was a suspicion, Lalli!' My protest sounded lame even to myself. Certainly, Lalli was guilty of murder.

'Look at all the facts, Sita: I failed to prevent a murder. I suppressed evidence. After all this, I could still have pursued the case. I didn't—'

'You did go to Munira—who exactly was she?'

'Long story, but all I'll tell you now was that the police employed her as a sketch artist. Her work was in demand—computers were still light years away from the Bombay Police. We got to be friends. It saddened me to learn she had died of cancer a few years ago. I wish I had kept in touch.'

'Why did Munira keep the picture?'

'I never went back for it. I never met her after that. The pressure of guilt and responsibility was so intense, I had erased the case from my mind by the end of the year. And that's not all, Sita.'

'There's the why of it.'

'Why did I commit this crime? I went out of my way to suppress it. This woman was an apparent stranger—or was she? For the life of me I couldn't remember. For the life of me I didn't want to remember.'

'What now?'

'I have to find her.'

'Lalli! After seventeen years? You're going to Kanyakumari now?'

'Oh, I hope not. I'm not fit to travel. Besides, I think she was from Bombay.'

'What makes you say that?'

'Eh? I just know.'

'No, Lalli. You know for a reason.'

'*Because I knew her in Bombay.*' The words shot out of my aunt, jolting both of us.

'I can't remember where,' she said, after a long silence. 'But I can hear her voice. *Singing*.'

'A Dikshitar *kriti*?'

'Yes! But she sang it differently. And the murder was because of the song.'

That made no sense at all. How could singing a song 'differently' in Bombay be the motive for murdering a man in Kanyakumari? A man, moreover, who wasn't singing?

No, I had it. In a brilliant flash of intuition I had the solution.

'It happened like this,' I said slowly. 'This woman who sang "differently" was due to perform at the Navaratri Kutcheri, but this priest prevented her in some way. Maybe he raised some sort of objection, he got in her way.'

Lalli shook her head. 'I wish it were that simple. Still, I'm in hopes of remembering more. It's been a relief telling you this, Sita. I'm for a nap now.'

She had ended our conversation sooner than I wished.

Lalli's phone rang. I froze, dreading the news from the hospital.

'No, that's not possible. You can bring him here. Around five? See you then.' Lalli grew absolutely still, her eyes distant. 'That was Shukla. Ramachandran's about the same. We can expect Subbu Bhagavathar here at five.'

'Here? Why not the chowki?'

'Because I don't feel up to going to the chowki today. I think I'll rest for a while now.'

Lalli's revelations had disturbed me more than I was willing to concede. I understood her hesitation now, about confiding in Savio. He would have gone straight to Kanyakumari, hunted down Jacob and reopened that file.

I was more than a little irritated by her decision to see Subbu Bhagavathar here. No doubt Shukla's phone call had been about releasing Senthil's body. I didn't see why Lalli should intervene in procedure. It would mean an unpleasant and certainly a very difficult encounter.

Poor Senthil—no, I withdrew that. However painful his brief life had been, he had achieved not just joy, but inspiration in his distorted reality. And was it distorted? What vision had he seen?

Layam

Shukla arrived, as promised, at five.

The Subbu Bhagavathar who faced Lalli this evening was very different from the curmudgeon we had met earlier. His flabby face had crumpled, his eyes were wary with anxiety, not belligerence. However heartless he had seemed towards his son, there was no mistaking his grief now. His voice too was pitched an octave lower.

'When we met the other day, I didn't know who you were. I beg your pardon if my manner offended in any way,' he began ingratiatingly.

'Not at all. Please sit down. Inspector Shukla mentioned you had something important to say. As you know, we have our reasons for not releasing Senthil's body just yet. The investigations will take another twenty-four hours, at least.'

'That is his destiny. He has earned it. What more can I say? It's not about the body that I wish to speak, although what I have to say might help your investigations. What are you investigating? What will his body tell you?'

'The cause of death.'

'Epilepsy. You know that already.'

'In fact, we don't.'

'What! He suffered all his life from fits!'

'All the more reason why it's strange he should die of it. Besides, there are many other causes for fits besides epilepsy. The first tests we did suggested he might have a brain tumour. Now we'll know for certain.'

'How does that concern the police? Surely it's a matter for doctors. Yes, my son was a criminal. You arrested him. He is dead. Your job is over.'

'No it isn't. We can only close the file when the cause of death is established beyond doubt. It will also tell us if Senthil was guilty of murder.'

'That's what I want to speak to you about.'

'So you no longer believe in Senthil's guilt?'

'No, that cannot be denied, but he may have been influenced, goaded, to assault his uncle. That is what I fear. And now my own life is in danger.'

He took a grimy towel from his bag and mopped his face. He asked for a glass of water.

As I rose to get it, Lalli intercepted me. 'Sita, get your notebook, this may be important.'

Never before had she asked me to take notes. Mystified, I obeyed.

'You were saying your life is in danger?'

'Yes, it is. I haven't slept a wink since I realized that. Last night, around eight o'clock, my son Guru paid me a visit.'

'Where?'

'The temple has kindly given me shelter. Guru came there.'

'Please continue.'

'It was not our first meeting. We had seen each

other once, but not spoken. I became emotional. I tried to embrace him. He assaulted me.'

'Assaulted you? How?"

'I find it difficult even to say the words. He kicked me. I fell down. He stood over me, threatening me. He said if I spoke a word about him to the police, he would kill me.'

'And yet here you are, talking with us,' Lalli said admiringly

'It's my duty.'

'So what is it that Guru forbids you to say?'

'The truth.'

'About why he ran away?'

'How did you know that? You must be a very clever detective to find out.'

'I haven't found out the truth. I'm waiting to hear it from you.'

Subbu Bhagavathar mopped his brow again and fanned himself with his mel veshti. Lalli shot me a warning look that made me subside in my chair.

He broke into Tamil. 'The other day, you asked me about my wife. I'm afraid I didn't tell you the truth. She didn't die of a fever. She was poisoned. Guru poisoned her.'

'At the age of seven?'

'Yes. I tried telling myself the child didn't know what he was doing, but how long can a father hide the truth from himself?'

Subbu hid his face in his mel veshti and howled.

No other word will describe his noisy sobs. Shukla, who had effaced himself for so long, began to show signs of impatience. Lalli quelled him with a look.

Finally, Subbu composed himself and gave us the story.

His wife had a cough, for which she took a syrup at bed time. Guru was a naughty and violent child. He had got into a fight with Senthil and knocked him about. The mother had punished him.

'I'll show you,' Guru threatened her. 'After that you'll never be mean to me again.'

That night, the mother took her cough syrup as usual—it was vile smelling stuff and she always held her nose when she took it.

Two hours later, she was in agony. On the way to hospital, she died.

'See, I told you I'll fix it so that she'll never be mean to me again,' Guru gloated.

'And he was only seven! What could I say!' Subbu wailed. 'I smelt the bottle—it stank of insecticide. I ran to check the tin that was kept in the bathroom shelf. It was empty.

Guru stood watching me. He said, 'It kills cockroaches very fast, so I thought it would kill her quickly and it did, didn't it?'

'God forgive me, I beat him black and blue. In the morning, he was gone. Yes, I did try very hard to find him, but in the depths of my soul I was glad. I had fathered a demon—what can I say?' Subbu shuddered.

'Who else knows this?' Lalli asked.

'Nobody. How could I tell anyone? I couldn't tell Inspector Shukla here. A secret can be told only in one's own tongue. So I requested a meeting with you.'

Subbu's narrative had been bilingual enough for Shukla to stay on board. Now he asked, 'What about your brother? Did he know the story?'

'No. And I have no idea when he met Guru. It couldn't have been very long ago, Narayanan had no secrets from me. He was a wayward fellow, but open-hearted. But I can tell you if he had known the story, he wouldn't have kept quiet. He had great regard for my wife.'

Subbu took another break in his mel veshti. He spoke through its folds, his voice muffled: 'Now you understand why I'm worried about Senthil as well.'

'Meaning?'

'Guru was with Senthil the night before he died.'

'So?'

'He may have poisoned Senthil.'

'What for?'

'To keep him from telling.'

'You think Senthil knew Guru poisoned their mother?'

'When it happened—certainly! He tried to stop me when I was beating Guru. He heard everything. All these years I taught him Thevaram hoping the holy words would make him forget. I thought I had succeeded. But—perhaps when he saw Guru, he remembered everything.'

'You saw Senthil yesterday morning. How was he then?'

'He complained of a severe headache. I went there early because he must drink his kashayam at daybreak, or the vaidyan says it won't act. So he drank it, and recited the *kavacham* with me, as usual. Then I left.'

'What did he say about the murder?'

'Nothing. And I did not ask him.'

'Was he happy to see you?'

'Relieved, I think. He asked after my head injury. He charged me to take my medicines. Poor child! He always took good care of me.' And back went Subbu into his mel veshti again.

'This is a very serious allegation, Shukla,' Lalli announced. 'Please do the needful.'

'Needful will be done,' Shukla assured her.

'What about me?' Subbu quavered. 'What if he attacks me?'

'Inspector Shukla will protect you,' Lalli cooed. 'But Shukla, what about Ramachandran? I'm really worried about him now. Guru's there with him. You know Ramachandran, I think, Bhagavathar?'

'Yes, we've met, he was very kind to my Senthil. At that meeting I had no idea he was a musician! Now that I know, I'm very eager to meet him, but I hear he's had a heart attack. Sivasiva, only good men are tormented like this!'

'Oh but he's getting so much better,' gushed my aunt.

'Then please permit me to visit him once he's allowed visitors,' Bhagavathar said. 'We will have a lot to talk about. He was with my son at the end.'

'I must warn you not to talk of that when you visit him,' Lalli said. 'He is still in a delicate state.'

'Of course, of course. We will talk music. I will be happy to see him at my Harikatha. You also, madam. Bring your daughter, young people need such enlightenment. I will let you know the date of my next performance. You also, Inspector Shukla. I will sing Tulsidas specially for you.'

Lalli professed herself delighted, and Subbu Bhagavathar prepared to take his leave, restoring the grimy towel to the bag and the saturated mel veshti to his shoulder.

'My poor wife—I'm glad she is dead,' Subbu said. 'All this would have made her miserable.'

'True, very true,' Lalli sighed. 'Kamala would have been brokenhearted.'

Subbu Bhagavathar stopped in his tracks. 'You know my wife's name!' he said wonderingly.

'Eh? Why, you mentioned it at least a dozen times in the last half hour,' Lalli retorted.

'He didn't, Lalli,' I said as the door closed on Subbu Bhagavathar and Shukla.

'Didn't what?'

'Mention his wife's name. Not once.'

'He didn't?' Lalli frowned. 'Then how did I know it?'

Subbu Bhagavathar's visit had agitated Lalli. She paced about the house with fierce energetic strides as though her legs were steel springs. I didn't dare attempt conversation. Dinner was a meal-in-a-bowl and she ate hers walking.

'Dr Q's late,' she frowned. 'He said eightish.'

'Oh. Should we have waited dinner?'

'No, no. I hope Shukla got everything.'

'More or less, I think he did. Subbu spoke Hindi half the time. He's the original Shaktivel.'

'I didn't mean what Subbu said. I hope Shukla got what I said.'

'About Ramachandran?'

'Yes.'

'Lalli, can a child of seven knowingly commit murder?'

'Depends on what you mean by "knowingly". Children have a different reality, and therefore, their moral understanding is different from the adult one.'

'Have you ever known a child to commit murder?'

'Yes. Quite a few, in fact. And some of them were perfectly aware of the consequences of the act.'

'What happened to them?'

'The worst that can happen to a child. They were tried as juveniles and put into the state-run institutions that practically manufacture criminals.

There are no resources for children in our country. No food, no shelter, no education, no parental protection, no rights. Despite all this—they shine. Until they find their slots and become their parents all over again. Look at these two—Senthil and Guru.'

'I won't say they're particularly shining examples of anything, Lalli. One died a murderer. The other was one to start with.'

'Really? I hadn't noticed.'

It's not often that Lalli gets mad at me—in fact I can't remember the last time that happened, but it was sure as hell happening now.

Luckily, Dr Q chose that moment to ring the doorbell.

'Sorry I'm late. Looked in on Ramachandran, status quo there. I got talking with Guru—listening to him, rather. This case has filled my skull with music and I can't decide whether it's torment or pleasure.'

'If it's Guru, it's likely to be torment,' I said, and told him Subbu Bhagavathar's story.

'So what did you find, Dr Q?' Lalli demanded edgily. 'Organophosphorus poisoning? Just in case Guru's kept up his childhood weakness for insecticide.'

'Slow down, ladies. Sita, give me something to eat, I'm starving—no, I must have dinner at home, but a cup of coffee, perhaps?'

He just wanted me out of the room. He picked up

the newspaper and sat down in his usual armchair. Lalli stopped pacing, though she still drifted about. A little later, I heard her pull up a chair at the table.

'Whatever it is, you're not responsible,' I heard him say.

'You wouldn't say that if you knew the truth.'

'Do you?'

'Almost. And I am responsible for—everything.'

'We'll see.'

'You may not be around to see, Dr Q. Once you learn the truth, you may not want to be around.'

He didn't answer that, so I took in the coffee with a slice of gingerbread.

It's always a pleasure offering Dr Q food or drink—he accepts it like a benediction that's morally elevating for the cook.

'No signs to suggest insecticide poisoning, toxicology reports will be in tomorrow morning. But the brain—ah.' He set down his cup. 'You remember what Shah thought was a "tumour"—possible hippocampal sclerosis on MRI? And the EEG showed an anterior temporal spike? Well I sectioned the brain.'

'Nothing?'

'Exactly. Of course, the final verdict will be on microscopy.'

'Clinically, temporal lobe epilepsy fit the bill until I actually witnessed a seizure.'

'Poisoning? None of the usual suspects. But

we're looking here at the cause of a sudden abrupt change in consciousness, arousal and sudden death. Many poisons that could cause that are eliminated completely from the body within twenty-four hours. The sudden death though, had a visible explanation.'

'Octopus pot?'

'Exactly.'

Definitely, time to intervene. 'You didn't actually say Octopus Pot, did you?' I asked.

'I did, I can't remember the Japanese term for it,' Lalli assured me mystifyingly.

'Takotsubo. It describes the shape into which the apex of the heart is distorted. The condition also has a more romantic term—broken heart syndrome.'

'You're kidding, Dr Q!'

'Far from it. Sudden cardiac stoppage following emotional shock. Common in elderly women, not unknown in the very young. As I was saying, Lalli, typical appearance—both on naked eye and microscopy. Yes, Sita, one can now legitimately die of shock. A huge surge of adrenaline and—pop!'

'So if he was poisoned, he recovered from the poisoning,' I put it together slowly. 'He woke up, didn't he? He talked coherently with us. And then he had that vision—and it killed him!'

Their silence told me I was right.

'Shukla should be able to give you something by mid morning tomorrow,' Lalli told Dr Q.

'Right. I'll rush it through, never fear.'

And with this mystifying exchange, Dr Q left.

'I'll be out early tomorrow, Sita, but I'll need you after lunch if that suits you,' Lali said.

And in an uncharacteristic gesture, she bent and kissed my cheek. I felt her tears sting me. Inexpressibly moved, I stared wordlessly as she left the room.

The day began with my publisher trashing a manuscript: *Too niche, and the market's a beast*, her note said. Savio was lost somewhere in Vashi, depriving me of a truly volcanic vent.

It didn't help at all when Manda Tai and Patherphaker rang the doorbell at eleven, looking more self-righteous than usual. I had seen them leave in a taxi at seven, presumably to the hospital.

'Oh *he*'s all right!' Manda stated, implying that *they* were not.

I invited them in, and set the kettle, the Patherphakers being connoisseurs of that Mumbai staple, kadak chai.

'Six o'clock we have left the house,' Manda said in an aggrieved tone. 'Not even one khari he has eaten. Quickly quickly I have made kanda pohe and thermos with Nescafe and my mister has run out in search of taxi. But what's the use? Ponni is like my sister, you know that, Sita.'

I nodded into the significant pause. 'Up till now,' she finished.

'Ultimately, you know, Sita, when it comes to

the final reckoning, people revert to their own,' Patherphaker said bitterly. 'Hindu will go with Hindu, Mussalman with Mussalman, North with North, South with South. It is the law of the jungle. From today I'm changing. I'm now Savarkar bhakt.'

This was serious. Patherphaker loathed the RSS and all it stood for. He had once interrupted Ponni when she sang the heartrendingly lovely *O sagara* saying if she was going to sing Savarkar's song, he was leaving.

I brought in the tea and cravenly poured a cup for myself in a gesture of solidarity, wondering what Ponni had done to betray their friendship.

'She's gone!' Manda announced. 'Just like that! To her sister's place.'

'I didn't know she had a sister,' I said.

'She does not. Of that I am sure. We know each other's family history, every particle, good or bad. There is no sister.' And putting down her cup, Manda crossed her arms and glared.

'No, no, we cannot be certain.' Patherphaker dipped a biscuit delicately in his tea. 'She has written in her note, sister within brackets cousin. We are aware of immediate family of both Ramu and wife, but within brackets relations are unknown. Still, I'm telling Manda, we cannot blame Ramu. Poor fellow.' Patherphaker rose and went to the balcony, overcome.

'They are like this, my mister and Ramu.' Manda

clasped her hands together. 'Nothing can tear them apart. But this was unexpected from Ponni. Give me the recipe of this cake, later, okay? He does not eat eggs, but why tell?'

Ponni, it transpired, had left Ramachandran to his fate and gone to her cousin's place in Dombivli as the doctors had decided that Ramachandran needed two more days of recuperation before they could decide on the next step of treatment.

Anyway he is eating hospital food and sleeping most of the time, Ponni's note read, *and I certainly need some rest.*

'Usually, she is putting him first,' Manda said sadly. 'Only when such things happen we come to know the truth. Who is this cousin sister? Where she has come from all of a sudden? Now my anger has passed, I'm worried, Sita. So we thought we should let Lalli know.'

Guru, in permanent attendance outside the ICU, had handed the Patherphakers Ponni's note. No, he hadn't seen her leave. Inspector Shukla had asked him to show up at the morgue as some details on Senthil's form were needed, and when he returned, he found Ponni gone. The ICU Sister had given Guru the note.

'Why Inspector Shukla asked Guru and not the father about Senthil's details?' Patherphaker demanded. 'He knows Guru has just turned up, no contact with family for so many years. Even we know this. So how can Guru help with details? Also I have questioned all the nurses very closely, following CID technique.'

Manda nodded. 'In that he is perfect. Not single episode he has missed till now. He is watching all the crime shows, each and every.'

'And?' I prompted Patherphaker.

'Nobody saw cousin sister. Ponni gave the note and left. We do not know with whom.'

'Her phone is switched off,' Manda added.

'Very significant,' Patherphaker said.

'Ramu should know,' Manda declared. 'Better he knows now before it is too late.'

'What do you mean?' I asked. 'Too late for what?'

'You are still young,' Patherphaker observed darkly. 'The ways of the world are still strange to you.'

'Not at thirty-six!' I protested.

'Maybe, but you are trusting. Savio will understand. Tell him if you think Lalli is too weak to be troubled now. Where is she?'

'I wish I knew,' I said. 'This case is too much for her to take just now.'

Why did I say that? It was manifestly untrue, yet the words had shot out, catapulted by anxiety.

'She will be all right,' Patherphaker assured me blithely. 'She is always all right.'

'But she will not be all right about Ponni,' Manda rose to go.

I promised to tell Lalli about Ponni's defection. I carefully restrained myself from expressing my own opinion. Ponni needed space to think. There was no cousin. She had lit out for air.

Lalli returned as promised, around lunchtime. She had little appetite, but I blackmailed her into eating something. Her opinion about Ponni's disappearance was much like my own.

'Where are we off to now?'

'Matunga.'

Tamizhagam in Bombay is much more diverse than the curious Sunday Supplement dichotomy of Tam Brahm and Chettinad. The one place to view the entire spectrum is at the provision store. (No, not the customers—the hoi polloi are practically indistinguishable from the chosen, until they place their orders. *Then* it's a dead giveaway. They point to the display and say, 'That.')

Tamizhagam *is* the display, from the literature section at the entrance (panchangam, matrimonials, magazines, newspapers), to the open sacks at the back where you must venture if you're picky about hand-pounded rice, red chillies and tamarind.

The crowded midsection is the most variegate. Here the pickled, the preserved, the dessicated, and the fossilized jostle with the day's arrivals, crisp or sugary in plastic cauls. Here are mysterious compounds you can spend a whole afternoon analyzing after a single whiff, and still miss out an ingredient or two. The atmosphere is a mixture of roasting coffee beans, red chillies, jute, newspaper, camphor and jasmine—the last two from a satellite stall on the pavement.

It was to one such store that Lalli led me in Matunga market. As I pottered blissfully, discovering forgotten delights like vepillai katti and mahani, checking out the range of pickles and pappadam, Lalli had accumulated enough merchandise for a family of ten and was now enjoying a leisurely chat with the shopkeeper

'Oh yes, Ruku Mami's elai vadam was famous, people came from as far away as Goregaon just for it. The stock was sold out by afternoon. That was in my father's time.' He pointed cheerily to the deceased, now an icon garlanded with sandalwood.

'I remember your father very well. So Ruku Mami also—'

'Ten-fifteen years ago. But her daughter supplies everything as before. Except the famous elai vadam—that she says is beyond her!'

'Her daughter? Oh, now I remember. Sukanya, right?'

'You do have a good memory. Sukanya is right!'

'I would love to meet her. Perhaps she takes orders? For my son in the US.'

'New Jersey?'

'California.'

'Ah. Yes, Sukanya lives nearby, I'll give you her mobile number.'

Ten minutes later, weighed down with Lalli's parcels for the mythical Californian, we trudged up three steep flights in a dingy old building behind the shopping arcade.

'I remember this place now,' Lalli gasped. 'I could have saved a lot of time if I'd remembered earlier. Here, this is the house.'

The usual nondescript door was festooned with mango leaves, dried and cobwebbed, souvenirs of long ago festivity. The kolam on the threshold, once a plastic sticker, had grown blurry like an ancient tile, embedded in a permanent film of grime. The air sagged with a memory of heating oil.

The woman who opened the door peered at us with a wavering smile, narrowing her myopic eyes.

'Sukanya, you don't recognize me, I see,' Lalli smiled.

'Lalli!'

She drew us in with a glad cry of welcome that sounded musical in her sweet voice. She was in her fifties, a slender woman whose anxious face seemed even more on edge from the fierce discipline on her hair. There was a lot of it, oiled and twisted into a chignon quilled with pins. Her face lost most of its strained lines once she had found her spectacles.

"There, now I recognize you perfectly. You haven't changed a bit.'

'I was sorry to hear about Ruku Mami.'

'Diabetes. What can I say! I see you've come from the store. Ganesh must have given you directions—'

'Yes, but once I got to the lane, I remembered well enough.'

'Ah, but what made you remember me, Lalli? Or my mother?'

The question, quick and direct showed the realist behind the scatty façade. Perhaps the pincushion on her head should have told me that earlier.

'Are you still with the police? Is this your daughter? No—you were single, must be your niece. And you must be retired by now.'

'You're as good a detective as I am,' Lalli smiled. 'You're right, I'm here seeking your help on a case.'

Sukanya looked flattered. She suggested coffee. The tiny room we sat in was once the vestibule of the small flat. Now it served as a bedsit. The rest of the house had been turned into a kitchen. Sukanya was back in a few minutes with steaming tumblers of coffee and a plate of kai murukku.

'Just made this batch, so tell me what you think.' She offered me one perfect four-tiered twisty whorl. It snapped with alacrity, exhaling a toasty whiff of sesame.

'Sukanya, do you remember that music master? The one your mother recommended? I've been trying to trace him. Can you help?'

'Who? You're not asking me about poor Kamala's

husband by any chance, are you? Mani Vadyar? At one time Amma used to recommend him, but that was long ago, before the trouble started.'

'Oh?'

Sukanya shot me a bright enquiring look.

'Perfect,' I assured her. 'Delicious.'

'So strange you should ask me about him, today of all days, when I've made kai murukku. This season's all hot work, you know, bent over oil all day. I wait for May! It's my coolest month! As I was saying, Kamala's kai murukku was famous, only everyone thought it was my mother's. She used to bring two large tins every week and leave it for my mother to send over to the store. Times were hard, but it was beneath Mani Vadyar's dignity to let his wife earn her living. But Kamala fried the murukku in coconut oil. I use rice bran, so much healthier.'

'You mentioned poor Kamala had troubles.'

'Oh no, not Kamala, that was a terrible tragedy. The trouble was about the students, so many of them left. The class would be full for a few months, and then the children would just stop coming. Really sad. He was quite famous, you know.'

'Oh? He performed at kutcheris?'

'Yes. I've heard him once or twice. I didn't think much of him, quite a nasal voice. Now Kamala, she was a different matter altogether! Poor Kamala.'

'She was a musician too?'

'Lovely voice, sweet as a flute, but he wouldn't

let her sing. So she played the violin, used to accompany him. And then suddenly—' Sukanya made an annihilating gesture. 'Isn't it strange how life changes in an instant? We heard about it only later. We were in Madras for a wedding, a relative's wedding, worse luck, all work, no pay. We slaved making laddu and athirasam and five sorts of paruppputengai. Nobody does all that now, they just buy from these big shops. But wait, you'll never guess who makes paruppputengai—Master Chef! They call it crocksomething, but it's paruppputengai made out of small biscuits. Saw it the other day. Crocksomething.'

'Croquembouche,' I offered.

'Yes, that's it! Same conical moulds, but who wants to eat biscuits in syrup? Yuck.'

Lalli hauled her back to the music master's tragedy, with some difficulty.

'Ah yes, the tragedy. The girl died. Sleepwalked right off the balcony. That's what we heard.'

'Kamala's daughter? How old was she?'

'Twelve or thirteen. Eighth or ninth standard. She died, and the very next day Kamala developed high fever and she died too, poor thing.'

'Terrible. What did the poor man do?'

'What could he do with two small children to look after? He went back to their village, some small place near Madurai, so I heard. I'm a Bombay girl, so apart from Madras, I don't know any place in Tamil Nadu.'

'And what did your mother think of all this?'

'Oh she was her usual self, you knew her!' She gave a mirthless laugh, which my aunt echoed.

'Now, that was what I call a good afternoon,' Lalli said smugly as we drove home.

The back seat overflowed with parcels. Lalli had bought lavishly at Sukanya's, pickles, pappadam, podis.

'What are we going to do with all this food, Lalli?' I wailed at the thought of having to conjure up dishes to go with this orchestra of accompaniments.

'Oh? The crisps will be good for Shukla, and the pickles will console the Patherphakers. Don't let it burden your soul.'

'Lalli, let me get this straight—you think this Mani Vadyar has something to do with the case?'

'What did Subbu Bhagavathar say his wife's name was?'

'Kamala—no actually, he didn't. You did.'

'Yes, Sita.'

'So Subbu and Mani—'

'Are the same Subramaniam, yes.'

I digested this slowly. One horrific tragedy piled on another—and then the story that Subbu had given us about Guru. No wonder he had changed his name and given himself a new life. Subramaniam had started life as Mani and decided to finish it as Subbu. His sons had erased their childhood. To each, his way.

'Then he has more courage than I imagined,' I said. 'He's quite a creep.'

'Of sobs and tears he sorted out those of the largest size, holding his pocket handkerchief before his streaming eyes?'

'Exactly. People can't help what they are, but he's tremendously brave to have survived all that.'

'I don't place any value on survival,' my aunt said. 'It's the quality of life—and the quality of death—that I worry about.'

Left to my own thoughts that evening, I didn't see how the morning's events mattered to the case. No doubt Shukla had his eagle eye trained on Guru, but until Dr Q produced hard evidence of Senthil's being poisoned, there was nothing he could move on.

Savio called late to say he was still held up at Vashi.

Before I could tell him about my day, he said hurriedly, 'Tell Lalli I've got it,' and rang off.

Lalli smiled absently when I told her. She had retreated into her cocoon of isolation on the beige sofa, bright-eyed, watchful, still in intense concentration. She ignored dinner.

When I turned in at eleven, she said, 'Tomorrow's going to be a long day. Sleep late.'

I did.

The house was dead quiet when I woke. That meant Lalli was out.

I drank a gloomy cup of coffee in the kitchen, pondering the eternal conundrums:

When is a book a book?

When it is read.

When is a book not a book?

When it's read by a publisher.

There was more truth in that than any philosopher could dream up.

Misery had me by the roots.

I got up angrily and grabbed my notebook.

Five hours, and forty pages later, I was interrupted by the doorbell.

The clock's irritating cheep told me it was noon. I hadn't done a thing since I woke—or perhaps, I'd done the only thing worth doing.

And now here came life, preparing a Break & Entry.

It was Manda. 'Any news?'

'No, but Lalli said she'd be looking out for Ponni today,' I lied.

Manda was quite satisfied with that. 'Then Ponni is safe. These days you can never tell. Men are naturally suspicious. They have dirty minds.'

'Filthy.'

She came in to examine the pickles and pappadams and I sorted out a generous selection as she took in the comatose kitchen at a glance.

'I'm getting you late,' she gathered up her loot. 'You'll tell me if you hear from Lalli?'

'Immediately.'

'Patherphekar is worried, not slept one wink. What will happen to Ramu if he finds out, he keeps saying. Men have dirty minds.'

'Filthy!'

And on this comforting note of sisterhood, I wearily took up my day.

The house can be as much of a beast as the market some days, and this was one. Lalli has it muzzled by seven, but today it really turned around and bit me.

When Savio came in two hours later, I was actually sobbing. He extracted me grimly from a maze of abandoned chores and whisked me away to lunch.

Savio's favourite restaurant has recently morphed into a ribbed plastic bubble that bulges out on the pavement. It is completely see-through. Right from the manager's console to the onion mincers in the back kitchen, everything's flagrantly on display. The change in décor was enforced when the mezzanine reported 'morality issues' in its tenebrous alcoves.

The menu too has changed. Dosais and vadais have given way to pizzas and wraps.

Savio stared gloomily at his Chutney Jhatpat: a failed bun choked with a patty that oozed compost.

I bit nervously into my wrap. It had the consistency of vellum and tasted just as dead.

We ordered ice-cream.

'At least this won't have changed,' Savio brightened up.

But it had.

My misery peeled off as I subsided into giggles at the look on Savio's face when he examined the teaspoon of ice-cream floating in a muddy puddle of hot chocolate. It melted before his spoon could lever it out of the morass.

We went home and Savio cleaned up the house as I got a decent meal on the table. After an intensely pleasurable silence, I told Savio about our adventures yesterday.

'So that's what Lalli's been up to,' Savio grinned. 'We should get there by tomorrow, I think.'

'Get where?'

'To the bottom of this case. Subbu Bhagavathar is waiting for Shukla to tell him when he can visit Ramachandran. He says he has some special prayers he would like to chant at his bedside. The man's a terrible nuisance.'

'Pity him, Savio. He's had a hard life. And he's genuinely grateful to Ramachandran for the kindness he showed Senthil.'

'What's the use?' Savio got up. 'Senthil died, didn't he? I'm going to see what Shukla's found. You gave Lalli the message, didn't you?'

'Yeah, that you've got it. She seemed to know what you meant.'

'Good.'

'I don't.'

'Senthil's clothes.'

'Oh? Where did you find them?'

He smiled and gave me a brief hug. 'Where Lalli said they'd be. But you're devastated by what she's told you, aren't you?'

'I—I can't talk about it.'

'I know. She'll tell me soon enough. I know it's so bad you can't come to terms with it.'

He was right. I had never known Lalli to suppress the truth. I had come round to her point of view: she was guilty of murder.

'You're still mad she didn't tell you,' I countered.

'She didn't tell me because she knows I'll accept whatever it is. She doesn't have to prepare me.'

'You think that's what she's doing by telling me? Preparing me?'

'Don't worry about it.'

As usual, Savio's reassurance brought me an illogical amount of peace. So much so that when Lalli returned, I was quite content not to bring up the tragic story Sukanya had told us.

But Lalli alluded to it by saying her own case too was now nearly solved. 'Thanks to Sukanya!'

'How does Sukanya have a bearing on your murder?' I asked, unconsciously using the word.

'Ah. My *murder*. What reparation do you think I should make, Sita?'

'The dead man's family needs closure.'

'Jacob tells me they regarded his death as closure—Jacob's prime suspect was the son, a boy of sixteen. He had come to blows with his father on several occasions when he stopped him from beating up his mother. Apparently, the boy told Jacob, "I didn't do it, but if it means buying my mother peace for the rest of her life, I will willingly hang for the crime."'

'That doesn't justify the murder.'

'I didn't think it did. You haven't answered my question. What reparation?'

'You've told Jacob?'

'Naturally. Just before I told you. He's retired, I had some trouble tracking him down, but these things are so much easier nowadays.'

'So will he reopen the file?'

'I already have.'

'That's putting yourself in the line of fire.'

She looked startled. 'You thought I'd dodge?'

'Oh, I knew you wouldn't flinch at that, but I don't think your question has to do with due process. You used the word *reparation*.'

'Yes. Is reparation even possible?'

I had no answer to that.

'Anyway, that must wait until we have this case sorted out,' Lalli sighed. 'Meanwhile, this should suffice for both reminder and reproach.' She lifted off the small picture on the wall next to the window, and replaced it with another. It was the second portrait of the Kanyakumari woman, the one Shaheen had drawn. The ageing face sprang out from a muted background that seemed all wrong today.

'Shaheen's very good at getting a likeness, but her palette's lacking,' I observed. 'This dull grey-green background really doesn't cut it. And the sari should be nondescript, not the background.'

'Really? What colours do you think would look right?'

'Bright yellow, black, dark brown and a flare of blue and viridian.'

Lalli looked unreasonably pleased with my artistic vision. 'And the nondescript sari—what colour should that be?'

I shrugged. 'I hadn't really noticed. It was just—nondescript.'

I wondered why Lalli was staring at me so intently—but the phone rang and distracted me.

It was Shukla, for Lalli.

'Right. We'll be there by five-thirty,' I heard her say.

She turned to me with a contented smile. 'Get some sleep now. We leave at five tomorrow morning, Sita. It's time we closed this case.'

We were silent on the long drive through the sleeping city.

Savio awaited us in the hospital porch. We followed him through a side entrance to the service lifts.

As we alighted on the fifth floor, we caught sight of Shukla in earnest conversation with a girl who looked about twelve, but was probably twenty-five. Her face was keen and child-like behind enormous spectacles. She chewed gum and blew a bubble when Shukla introduced us.

'This is Leena. Bug Lady,' he explained.

It took me a long moment to figure out her presence had nothing to do with entomology.

'Rat chamber, cat chamber, all her work,' he whispered.

We followed them into a cubicle. The centre-piece was a computer screen that showed somebody's broad back. Leena the Bug Lady twiddled some controls and the screen now showed the inside of a curtained cubicle. On the bed, wired to a frightening array of monitors all flashing waves in green and blue, snored a human lump I slowly recognized as Ramachandran. He looked even more massive than usual against the snowbank of pillows. A black lace-edged eyeshade added a kinky touch to the green and white hospital couture.

'Why are we watching him?' I asked.

'Sssh.'

Ramachandran went on snoring, the lights on the surrounding displays kept flashing.

Then Subbu Bhagavathar entered.

'His fourth visit,' Shukla informed us. 'Every visit, one prayer, he said. Dawn prayer is most important.'

Subbu made himself comfortable on the bedside chair. He began muttering, shutting his eyes and rocking slowly.

'He is holy man,' Shukla said with a look of reproach at Lalli.

The holy man kept muttering, Ramachandran kept snoring, and the display kept flashing.

This was just a waste of time.

Then Subbu stood up suddenly, a man transformed.

He looked directly into the camera, his face a mask of absolute calm. Bending forward, he placed his forearm firmly across Ramachandran's neck.

Lalli, uttering an exclamation, was about to leave the room when two things happened on the screen.

Subbu pressed his arm down with visible force, his face showing the effort.

Almost at once Ramachandran surged up, and tearing Subbu off him, practically hurled him across the room.

Off came the kinky shades, and I got my first unobstructed view of Ramachandran's face.

It wasn't him.

Shukla and Savio had taken off, but Lalli intercepted them at the door.

'Your man is wired, isn't he? Caution him to be quiet. Let's hear what Subbu has to say.'

Subbu picked himself up fearfully, trying not to look at the furious figure bolt upright on the bed.

A nurse entered.

'Who is this man?' roared the patient.

'You are not Ramachandran!' spluttered Subbu.

'No, I'm Utpal Naik. Who are you? Why did you attack me?'

'Attack?' Subbu threw his hands out in protest. 'I thought you were my friend, Ramachandran. I bent over you to apply vibhuti on your forehead after saying a prayer and this is how you treat me? If you're so tough, what are you doing in the ICU?"

This was unanswerable, so Utpal Naik pulled on his kinky shades again, and turning his back on Subbu Bhagavathar, composed himself to sleep.

'Plenty of talent in the force these days,' Lalli observed. 'Now let's see what story Subbu has for us.'

Savio replayed the footage. Except for the frames where Subbu faced the camera, there was very little to prove him wrong. His arm could have crossed the man's neck as he was reaching past his bulging torso. There was nothing that could stand up in court against Subbu's words. The Bug Lady's expertise had been wasted.

'What about his earlier visits to Ramachandran? It was this guy all the time wearing those shades? No conversation?' It seemed a singularly myopic operation.

'Same fat fellow, same shades,' Shukla muttered. 'We told Subbu that Ramachandran was sedated, and he would sleep throughout. We didn't expect physical attack.'

Towards Shukla, Subbu Bhagavathar was indignation personified. He claimed he had been injured by the patient. He had been led into that cubicle on false premises. He had requested five minutes, only five minutes, with his good friend Ramachandran to say the Gayatri mantra at this sacred hour and what was the result? He was assaulted by an unknown assassin.

'Calm down, Bhagavathar,' Lalli approached him gravely. 'The confusion is not Inspector Shukla's fault. We were not informed that Ramachandran had been shifted to the operation theatre for surgery, and another patient had been given his bed. But I'm here on a more serious matter that concerns you.'

'More trouble? Oh, I've had enough!'

'It's hard for me to say this to you. Your son Guru is dead.'

Savio and Shukla stepped back to give Subbu enough room as he sank to the floor, clutching his head and groaning.

'He's—my Guru is—dead? What happened?'

'His body was found by a neighbour this evening. There was a bottle of bug poison at his bedside. It appears to be suicide.'

'It's just. It's right. How can I deny that I am relieved? Guru, my son, my son!' Subbu wailed, rocking in an agony of grief.

'Better go home now,' Shukla said. 'Jeep will drop you home. We will send jeep for you when body is ready.'

Shaktivel materialized out of thin air and escorted Subbu away. So he hadn't been taken off the case, after all.

I was so befuddled by the turn of events, I handed the car keys to Lalli and blanked out on the drive home.

'Guru has had a distressing cough all week,' Lalli remarked conversationally. 'It was thoughtful of Subbu to offer him some kashayam, but Guru turned it down. How ironic then that Guru's own bottle of cough syrup should be loaded with insecticide.'

'The bottle at his bedside?'

'The very same.'

Fear made me suddenly nauseous. I had a fleeting thought it might be all an elaborate hoax on Subbu Bhagavathar—but it wasn't. Guru was really dead.

'No he isn't,' Lalli said quickly reading my thought. 'It smelt odd, so he brought the bottle over to Shukla.The bottle was in his backpack. He's been living in that corridor since Senthil was admitted, so anybody could have tampered with it.'

I was so exhausted, I could barely drag myself upstairs.

'We'll leave soon after lunch, say at two? I've arranged for us to be there by three,' Lalli said.

'Where?'

'You'll see. Get some sleep, Sita, I'll cook. There's something more I have to tell you—but that can wait.'

As I walked past the picture of the Kanyakumari woman, I was struck once again by the incongruity of the background.

'It's all wrong,' I muttered. 'There should be a blaze of yellow just here—the peacock didn't have it, so maybe I just want that blue and viridian and it wasn't really there....'

'You saw her, didn't you?' Lalli asked quietly.

'Saw her? No, I've never seen her before.'

'Never mind,' said my aunt.

Lalli woke me at eleven. I had slept for three solid hours and my head felt like a lump of lead. I showered and staggered into the living room on autopilot.

Lalli, looking very elegant in a lilac sari I hadn't seen before, was sitting in the armchair in an attitude of complete repose. Eyes closed, hands resting lightly on the newspaper on her lap, she appeared to be fast asleep.

'Coffee's in the kitchen, get me a cup too, please Sita, and quickly. I have something to tell you before I lose courage.'

This is what she told me.

❁

Matunga, October 1988

That morning, it was Deepavali, the wrong day surely, to intrude on a household, but it was the only free morning she had.

Lalli had the address from Ruku Mami. She couldn't understand her own compulsion to return to a challenge she had failed repeatedly.

Like most children, she had learnt the rudiments of music from her mother. The lessons had ended when she was twelve, and never resumed. And now, thirty years later, the memory of her mother's voice compelled her to recover something of her music.

A few basics, perhaps an hour a week was what Lalli had in mind.

Ruku Mami said this man was good. Good or bad, any music teacher knew more than she did!

Mani Vadyar was engaged, but would be free any moment, his wife said.

She was a woman of Lalli's own age. She was in Deepavali finery, a new sari that exaggerated her baby bump. About twenty-four weeks gone, Lalli guessed.

Lalli made herself comfortable on the lovely paai spread out for guests.

Elsewhere in the house, Mani Vadyar was in full spate. His nasal tenor elaborated a passage of *Pakkala nilabaadi* with more persistence than skill.

Lalli's hostess returned with a plate of Deepavali

bhakshanam. Ignoring Lalli's protests, she urged her to sample the delicacies.

'Try the murukku,' she held out a small perfectly twisted golden whorl. 'How old is your daughter?'

'My daughter? No, no, I'm here for myself,' Lalli replied with some embarrassment. 'Just a few lessons—to brush up on *varnam*, a *keertanai* or two. I would like to learn some Dikshitar *kritis*, my mother used to sing them beautifully.'

She nodded, as if reading beyond Lalli's request, and understanding her compulsion.

'Listen, I'll be frank with you—Vadyar doesn't sing Dikshitar.'

Lalli understood the woman's unsaid thought.

'I could teach you a song or two if—' she smiled ruefully, patting her stomach.

'First baby?'

'No,' she laughed.

There was a sudden cascade of notes from Mani Vadyar.

'A complicated *niraval*,' Lalli observed.

'Sometimes it's difficult to tell if it's *niraval* or *varaval*,'[6] she retorted with a sardonic twinkle.

Lalli hastily suppressed a laugh. 'It's Kharaharapriya, isn't it?'

'Yes—ah, here you are!' Her face lit up as a plump little girl of about three came running into the room, almost tripping on her new blue pavadai.

---

6. *Niraval*: musical elaboration of a phrase; *Varaval*: fry

Lalli caught her just in time.

She snuggled against her mother and regarded Lalli gravely from clear round eyes outlined with kajal. With a quick pounce she picked up a murukku from the plate.

'Yes, that's Kharaharapriya, and this is my karakara-priya,' the mother laughed. 'Go on, show off your pavadai to this aunty.'

'This is my pattu pavadai,' the child said, and with a delighted giggle whirled around and sat down abruptly with the blue corolla ballooned about her.

Enchanted with the child's joy, Lalli clapped heartily.

'Look!' The child lifted up her skirt and displayed her silver anklets, stamping her feet to make them tinkle. 'Bells!'

'Ooh!'

Her mother knelt before her and began singing *Kanjadalayadakshi*. From the child's giggles, it was evident this was a familiar game. The mother sang it teasingly, with much antic exaggeration.

Kunjara gamane,
Mani mandita, manjula charane![7]

She broke off to pick up the child and cuddle her.

'Kamakshi will sing Dikshitar for you,' she said. 'Come, child, let the lady hear you.'

Kamakshi settled herself crosslegged, placing the murukku she was clutching on her lap.

---

7. She walks like the elephant,
With bejeweled hips and delicate feet.

Her mother quickly removed it, rubbing the silk to make certain it wasn't stained.

Lalli pushed the plate towards the child, but she shook her head and prepared to sing.

The mother's soft voice guided her for the first few notes, then she picked up the *swaram* on her own and sang the simple melody with surpassing sweetness.

Lalli, who hadn't heard *Shyamale meenakshi* before, was simply entranced.

'Enough! Stop that! Stop that at once!'

The man filling the doorway chilled the room into silence.

'No English music in this house!'

His eyes took in Lalli and elided over her, fastening a cold glare on his wife, which she returned with interest.

The little girl took the opportunity to fill her lap with murukku. This time her mother didn't stop her.

Mani Vadyar retreated, growling. His wife threw a rueful glance at Lalli. 'He's very particular,' she murmured.

Lalli diverted the child with a jumping bunny made from her kerchief, and in a few moments, took her leave. 'Perhaps I can drop by after you're comfortable with the baby,' she said. 'Next year, maybe?'

But she never did.

'It was watching the woman with her daughter that made me repress the memory,' Lalli said slowly. 'I knew no matter how many more children she would have, no matter whom else her life contained, this little child was sacred to her soul. Such intensity of love is given only once in a lifetime. That song was like a code—the words were addressed to her daughter, and not just playfully.'

Lalli sang the *pallavi*, and not playfully, stopping at the point where the song had been interrupted by Mani Vadyar:

Kanjadalayatakshi, Kamakashi!
Kamala manohari! Tripura sundari!
Kunjara gamane,
Mani mandita manjula charane.[8]

'Do you understand now, Sita, what I felt? I too had known such intensity of love, and I had lost it. Witnessing it in another showed me the depth of my loss. It was more than I could bear. It threatened to annihilate me. And so, I forgot the moment. I erased it for sheer survival, I lost it, as I had lost that love.'

She was recently bereaved that year—she could have meant her mother's love. But I knew she did not. Dr Q's words returned to memory: 'This—this other person.'

---

8. O Kamakshi, with eyes like lotus petals.
Kamala's delight,
Beauty of the three worlds!
With the gait of an elephant
With bejeweled hips and delicate feet.

'I forgot it all. I didn't remember that encounter when I saw her next.' She placed Munira's picture of the Kanyakumari woman on the table.

I gasped. 'That's Kamala?'

'Yes. That's Kamala. I saw her in Kanyakumari on 5th October 1995. According to the Municipal records, Mani Vadyar's daughter's death is registered as 1st October 1995.'

'Why would Kamala go to Kanyakumari four days after her child's death? And when did Kamala die? Sukanya evidently got the day wrong.'

'Ah. There's no record of Kamala's death, no certificate was issued.'

'But—Subbu said he didn't bring the body back from hospital, so they must have certified it.'

'Somebody must have, or the crematorium won't accept a body. We haven't managed to locate the certificate.'

'If you could locate the daughter's there is no reason why you can't find hers, unless Subbu managed some chicanery to protect Guru.'

'That's a possibility, yes.'

'It's more than just a possibility. Subbu tried to murder Ramachandran to keep him from divulging what Senthil might have told him. I think he's been trying to protect Guru all along. It doesn't matter to him that they've been alienated for years. Maybe it's motivated by the fear of shame, not paternal love. I think he'll do anything to keep from outing Guru.'

'Flawed logic.'

'Why?'

She shrugged and picking up her cup, walked to the kitchen to revive the cold coffee.

Shukla and Savio were late. Lalli had almost decided to leave when they turned up. Leaving them to lunch, Lalli said we should be back by five.

'Where are you going, Lalli?' Savio asked.

'On a Proustian journey.'

'No need to explain, Sita,' Shukla remarked. 'Shukla is knowing all about Proust. Famous writer who became famous dipping biskoot in own chai, and immediately going in reverse gear. See his kismet. Every day I am dipping biskoot in chai, daily reversing, but who wants to read about Shukla? All this I am learning from Dr Q as we are dipping good much biskoot together in hospital corridor. Now see *his* kismet. Profession is vulture, but nature is culture. Excuse, please, after this project I am constant poet.'

'Oh, I'll buy your book if you ever write it,' I assured him.

'See? We are still dentate. Same address you got from Shaktivel, Lalli? Very sticky man, Shaktivel, worse than Fevicol. How you got it from him? Never mind, forget I asked. Kanchpada, that's all I know.'

Kanchpada was easily found, but there was nothing remotely glassy about the road we turned into.

It was lined on both sides with small nondescript kiosks that gave way to decaying lots of derelict garages and factories. Further up the road, parked trucks and tempos suggested more active industry. What could Lalli be looking for in a street like this?

As I got out of the car, I spotted a blaze of colour beyond a squalid clutch of kiosks.

It was a small gopurum, the pantheon cavorting in multicoloured exuberance, proclaiming yet another outpost of Tamizhagam.

There are many such in the most hellish surroundings, amidst huts half submerged in permanent bogs of filth.

A rainbow gopuram, pyramid or decorated dome, asserts itself as a community centre, not just a place of worship. A last-ditch stand of tribal identity against the powerful suction of assimilation.

On this street too, there was no other visibly Tamil identity. The shops all had Bombay names, though none of them sought the Chhatrapati's aegis.

The men lounging about, the women walking kids home from school, were indistinguishable from the Mumbai meld.

But as we approached the gopuram, a large enclosure advertised itself as Mariamman Devasthanam. The pre-Vedic and the Vedic, usually at loggerheads, but now, as Shukla might put it, completely dentate.

The place was deserted, except for three teenage

boys intent on carrom at the far corner and an elderly woman setting out her flower stall. Her sari, worn the Tamil way, and the level gaze with which she met Lalli's enquiry, spoke of a slightly different relationship with the street. She made her living here, but this was not home. She was going back soon. Maybe she had been saying that for twenty years, but she meant to, one day.

Lalli bought a length of kadambam at an outrageous price.

'I'm looking for the lady who sells murukku,' she said. 'I know she lives here. Can you guide me?'

'What do you want with her?'

'What does one want with a woman who sells murukku?'

'So where did you taste her murukku?'

'At the festival. Panguni Uttiram, Ambarnath,' I burst out, my heart hammering with excitement.

The flower-seller's eyes swivelled between the two of us.

'You're quite right,' Lalli said. 'I'm not a fool to pay you fifty rupees for a string of kadambam. That was for information.'

'You could have got that for free.'

'Nothing comes for free.'

'You're not here to buy murukku.'

'Did I say I was?'

'So what does one want with a woman who sells murukku?'

'That is for her to tell you after I've spoken with her.'

'Well, she won't speak with you.'

'Why not?'

'She's mute, that's why.'

'Mute, but not deaf. I'll speak. She'll listen.'

'She's not been very well since she was affected during the festival.'

'Is that so?'

'We didn't expect her to start—'

'Shaking like that?' I realized it was me, asking that question.

'Yes! The spirit doesn't enter you unless you've carried a kavadi, but it came to her even though she was there only to sell her murukku. It was all His grace.'

'Truly so,' Lalli affirmed.

'I had the presence of mind to apply a little thiruneer to her forehead and that stopped her shaking. She was like one dead for an hour afterwards. There she is now, she has a coconut stall here. I will go tell her. She's easily startled, so it's better if I stay when you're talking with her.'

'Please do.'

'Lalli, I know her,' I whispered. 'I watched her having that fit. Just a nondescript woman, nobody would notice her in that whirl of yellow and peacock blue and suddenly—' I broke off as I understood Lalli's unspoken question.

'Yes, I was watching the peacock man, the Azhagan—'

'Who else was with him, Sita?'

I frowned, trying to induce the memory. 'The *kandar kavacham* was just over, a man was decorating the kavadi with jasmine and there was another man standing over the Azhagan, a young man in a white shirt and dark pants—*Senthil*! Lalli, that was Senthil, he must have stepped out just as he finished the kavacham.'

'Yes—that explains why you thought the background was all wrong.'

'The background?'

'Of the picture Shaheen drew. Kamala's picture.'

'Kamala—' I could hardly say the words. 'Then Kamala isn't dead?'

'Here she is, now. You found her, Sita!'

I! I had found nothing, I had done nothing. I had seen, forgotten, and recollected the synaesthetic moment without actually *remembering*.

Memory is a surreal landscape, treacherous, unreliable. How had Lalli managed to navigate it?

The flower-seller stood her ground as we approached the coconut stall.

'Kamala.'

If the name meant anything to the coconut seller, she made no sign. She rearranged her wares with slow concentration, never raising her eyes.

'That's not her name,' the flower-seller said loftily.

'Kamala, I'm going to ask your friend to go away now. You won't want her to hear what I have to say.'

'I'm not going,' the flower-seller glared.

Lalli flashed her badge.

The woman left.

The coconut-seller looked up for the first time.

It was remarkable how good a likeness Shaheen had achieved—except that this woman's face was lined deeper with anguish.

But the eyes that met Lalli's were calm.

Lalli's response was completely unexpected.

She sat down on the cement ledge next to Kamala.

In a very soft voice, she began to sing.

Kanjadalayatakshi
Kamakshi—

Her voice caressed each syllable with a playful note.

Kamala manohari
Tripura sundari—

Kamala uttered a wild cry and sank to the ground.

She crouched with her head in her hands, shuddering and groaning.

The flower-seller came hurrying back. I intercepted her hastily.

'She'll be all right, don't worry—'

'How can I not worry? Who is that lady? Police?'

'Yes.'

I looked back. Lalli was now seated a little distance away, next to Kamala on the ground. She looked as if she was prepared to stay there a long while.

At length, Kamala looked up. She spoke in a hoarse voice as if speech had grown rusty within her.

'How did you know?' she asked. 'Did the boys tell you?'

'No, but you will.'

Kamala's reaction surprised me. She got up and smoothed down her sari. 'Wait here. I'll get my things and come with you.'

The flower-seller came running up. 'Aaya spoke just now! I heard her speak! For twenty years we haven't heard a word from her. And you just opened up her throat. Who are you?'

'My name is Lalli. You've been a good friend to her—what's your name?'

'Mayamma.'

'Mayamma, she's coming with us now, but she'll be back. If she can't come back soon, I will be here tomorrow, at this time, to explain. Wait for me.'

'That I will, Amma. Take care of her.'

Kamala was back almost at once, carrying a small bag. She stopped to exchange a look with Mayamma. She gave her a small cloth purse that her friend accepted hesitantly.

'Wait!'

Mayamma tore off a length of jasmine and,

twisting a leaf around it, pressed it into Kamala's hand.

Not a word was exchanged, but everything was said.

Lalli drove away with Kamala, leaving me to find my way home. When I got there, I found Savio and Shukla had left, so I turned to my notebook.

An hour later, the page was still blank. All I could think about was Kamala.

Lalli hadn't been able to trace her death certificate for the most obvious reason of all—*she was alive*.

Why had Subbu Bhagavathar lied about his wife's death?

Why had he accused his seven-year old son of murdering her?

And Kamala—If she had murdered the pujari, what had led her to do it?

The incident Lalli recalled might have made her feel murderous—it had made *me* feel murderous—but feeling murderous is very different from committing murder.

On the 5th of October 1995, Kamala had left the temple, gone out and bought a knife, and then ambushed the pujari and stabbed him. Her intention to murder him had definitely been formed at the instant Lalli described—even if her motive was long-standing.

What happened after the murder? Why had she

moved into a new life, among new people, in a new place?

Was it because she didn't want to return home, or was it because she didn't want to return to her old life?

Her silence may have erased her past to others, but it had kept her old self alive. It had kept her crime alive.

Lalli looked exhausted when she returned.

'I owe you an explanation,' she said, but I insisted we have dinner first.

'I didn't say I was going to explain,' Lalli said. 'Enough of that tomorrow. Ramachandran's back home, did you know? The Patherphakers have forgiven Ponni. You've guessed by now that Shukla had them both moved after Subbu's visit here.'

'Lalli, why did Subbu lie about Guru? Kamala's alive, so Guru couldn't possibly have poisoned her—Lalli, I've got it!'

'Tell me.'

'It's terrible, really terrible! The daughter sleepwalks off the balcony and is killed. From the marriage you described, so acrimonious and bitter—Subbu—or at this point, Mani—and Kamala must have quarrelled. She walked out either volitionally or in a fugue. And then Mani discovered the insecticide-loaded cough syrup. He couldn't bear to tell the children their mother had abandoned them. He couldn't tell anybody that. That would shame him. So he gave out she was dead, and Guru gloated about the cough syrup. Mani thrashed him, and the child ran away.'

'That's one explanation, Sita.'

'Covers all the points, I think.'

'Yes. Except one. But don't worry about it. Tomorrow's going to be a very long day.'

I was a little surprised when Lalli asked me to do a couple of errands for her next morning. That would take me right across town. They didn't seem terribly urgent, and with a crowded evening ahead, there was a lot to be done in the house.

'Leave that to me, Sita. And we won't be having any refreshments, so there's nothing to be done,' she said airily.

The errands were soon done and I had an enjoyable morning, window shopping and lunching out with friends. I was planning to invade a bookstore when Lalli called to say they would be starting at four.

It was half past three already. I hit the road, more than a little irritated.

I heard voices as I got off the lift—so they had started without me.

They were all there—Dr Q, Savio, Shukla—and Ramachandran. Seeing him took the grouse out of me.

Lalli looked elegant in a simple magenta Kanjivaram. I caught a whiff of the dangerous perfume she reserves for difficult situations—magnolia, sandalwood, nutmeg, hint of pepper and rose.

'We're only waiting for Shaktivel to bring in Subbu Bhagavathar. We'll start the moment they arrive,' Lalli said.

The doorbell rang almost as she spoke.

'Very kind of you to come, Bhagavathar,' Lalli welcomed him. 'You know everyone here, I think?'

He started slightly when he noticed Ramachandran, and addressed his first words to him. 'I'm happy to see you looking so well, sir. I humbly beg pardon for all the trouble my poor son caused you.'

Ramachandran murmured a polite response. Subbu turned his attention to Lalli. 'It's very hard for a father who has lost both his sons to come to a gathering like this, to face a room full of strangers.'

'I understand, but we are not strangers to you. Please be comfortable. Here, let me take your bag.' Lalli picked up Subbu's black bag which he had placed on the floor, and put it on the table. Then, uncharacterestically, taking a chair at the far end of the room, she waited for silence. Her voice was low and very steady, but it was impossible to ignore the undertow of distress.

'We're here to close the file on Senthil. Let's begin with Narayanan's murder. He was killed around noon—his murder was reported at twelve-fifteen by the neighbour, Murthy, who discovered the body on hearing a loud cry. He found Senthil, in a bloodstained veshti and banian, standing over the fallen man. At a quarter to twelve, Senthil had left the temple, dressed in shirt and trousers. The walk takes ten minutes at a brisk pace. So we can presume Senthil reached home around noon. In the gap of fifteen minutes, three events occurred. Senthil changed his clothes. Narayanan was killed. Somebody cried out. Dr Q will you tell us please about the victim's injuries?'

'The murdered man could not have cried out. The skull showed many impacts with a heavy blunt weapon, but only one of these was antemortem. This impact, made with great force, shattered the back of the skull, and actually transected the medulla oblongata. It would have caused instantaneous death,' Dr Q said with quiet deliberation.

'Thank you. Inspector Shukla?'

'Senthil shouted. When we arrived on the scene, he was still shouting, doing bad-bad, looking wild. Immediately I called Sub-Inspector Shaktivel knowing Tamil, within five minutes he was on scene. Shaktivel?'

Shaktivel puffed out his chest. 'Accused was shouting, "Pita! Pita!" First I thought he was calling "Father! Father!" So I asked why have you murdered your father. He answered: This is not my father. Then he said again, he is not father, but aayan, something like that. Afterwards madam explained it is Pitta, not Pita, like that.'

'I'll explain that, it's integral to Senthil's personality,' Lalli said. '*Pitta, piraicchoodi perumane!* is the opening line of the devotional poem Senthil was used to reciting. The language of poetry was real to him. The familiar form of address to the Absolute made the poem an actual conversation Senthil had got used to. The gods and their leela, Thiruvilayadal, was real to him, much more real than the world that surrounded him. This was self-evident, so our first question was—is Senthil of sound mind? As it turns out, it was an irrelevant question. To return to what Shaktivel just told us, Senthil spoke in Tamil. He said "*Appan alla, aayan.*" Did Senthil sound bewildered as he said these words, Shaktivel? Dazed?'

'No, madam, he was very angry. It was paining him too much that time.'

'Excellent observation, Shaktivel. Those words caused Senthil intense pain. *Appan alla, aayan*. Not father, but Aayan. Ramachandran, enlighten us, please.'

'Aayan is the Tamil term for Brahma.' Ramachandran's rumble sounded more ominous than usual.

'Thank you, we'll return to that soon. On the morning of the murder, two events occurred in that brief time interval between Senthil's arrival and the discovery of the body. First, Senthil changed his clothes. Second, Narayanan was killed. Could both events have occurred in that short time? Yes, it's possible. After all, Narayanan was killed by a single swift blow which he never saw coming. There was no quarrel antecedent to the murder. He was killed in cold blood. What could have made Senthil do that?'

'My son was mental,' Subbu said. 'I have told you, I think, he was in Thana asylum for six months.'

'Yes, we know that. It would explain the attack, but not the change of clothes. Savio?'

'The clothes Senthil came home wearing were not found in the house.'

'So what? Clothes are kept in the cupboard. Senthil was very careful about these things,' Subbu retorted.

'Very careful,' Savio agreed. 'So careful that all the clothes in the cupboard are washed and ironed. None of those clothes were worn recently.'

'Side issue,' Subbu declared.

'Perhaps. Let us see, what do we have here? Savio, what is this?'

Savio had produced a bag identical to Subbu's. He now placed it on the table next to the bag Lalli had taken from Subbu.

Savio said, 'This is Subbu Bhagavathar's bag.'

'No, no, my bag's the one you first put on the table.'

'Let's see, shall we?' Lalli smiled. She reached for

the bag Subbu had brought and laid out its contents: panchangam, sandalwood, tins of kumkumam, vibhuti, turmeric, coconut, betel, paan, a small blow pipe, small black folding umbrella, plastic bag—

'In this season, I always carry a change of clothes,' Subbu explained.

'Exactly. Savio, check your bag, please.'

The contents were identical, down to the plastic bag.

'Now, what clothes do you expect to change into?' Lalli asked conversationally, shaking out her packet.

Subbu shook his head in a dazed manner.

'Let me see—veshti, angavastram, shirt. Right?'

'Yes, yes, that's it,' Subbu agreed.

'Savio?'

Savio shook out his packet. Out tumbled a pair of dark trousers and a white shirt.

'That's not my bag. Those are not my clothes. They're not even my size,' Subbu said angrily.

'It is your bag. Inspector Savio switched it with an identical one yesterday. It is your bag, but I agree, these are not your clothes. And yes, they're definitely not your size. Savio?'

Savio next produced a small tin.

'This is the medicine Senthil was given every day since his fits began.'

'Yes, made into a kashayam. Prescribed by a very famous vaidyan as I told you.' Subbu, relieved we were past the wardrobe controversy, prepared to be voluble. Lalli cut him short.

'You also told us the vaidyan's name, so we gave him this tin, and he denied having prescribed what it contains. What does it contain, Dr Q?'

'A number of psychotropic substances I won't name, but almost all of them are from common plants. The extract, prepared in the laboratory, induces hallucinations, convulsions, bizarre changes in mood.'

'I don't know all that. It's the medicine Senthil took all his life. It did him no harm,' Subbu wailed. He grabbed his mel veshti at the ready.

'True. You also made certain he got his morning dose the day before he died.'

'Yes. I was certain it would make him better.'

'But it didn't. However, its effects wore off, and Senthil was conscious and coherent a few hours before death. Why did he die, Dr Q?'

'Sudden cardiac arrest. Shock, you could call it, caused by severe emotion.'

'Sita and Ramachandran were both with Senthil at that time. Sita, can you tell us what happened.'

With some trepidation about the effect the recall may have on Ramachandran, I began. 'Senthil asked for a song, he asked for a song that would invoke Murugan—'

'And, Ramachandran, you sang—'

'A *thillana*. *Va, velava vadivelava mayil meedu va....*'

'At that point, Senthil, in great excitement called out Arumuga! Arumuga! Then he said Arumugan could not save him from the five-faced one, Ainthumugan—'

'Ramachandran, enlighten us, please.'

Ramachandran's voice sank an octave and boomed out, 'Brahma has five faces.'

'Only four,' Shukla protested.

'No, Inspector Shukla. The legend says he started out with five, and Siva knocked off one, leaving him, as you say, four-faced.'

'And nobody knows that legend as well as you do, Bhagavathar,' Lalli smiled.

Subbu Bhagavathar mopped his face with his mel veshti.

'And then, Sita, what happened next?'

'Then Senthil's eyes were fixed on something only he could see. His face grew radiant. He cried out "Amma!" The next moment, he stopped breathing.'

'So what did Senthil see?' Lalli demanded.

Silence answered her.

'It's the key question in this case. Senthil's vision really is the answer to the puzzle, and we will answer that by and by. But meanwhile, something else happened, didn't it, Bhagavathar? Guru threatened to kill you.'

'Yes, poor boy. I don't want to bring that up, now that he has finally paid for his sin.'

'And what sin was that?'

'I've told you.'

'We would like to hear it again.'

'You want to torment me. So be it. Guru poisoned his mother when he was seven years old. My wife died. When I thrashed him, Guru ran away. Senthil's fits began soon after that.'

'A tragic tale. How many children did you have, Bhagavathar.'

'Two sons.'

'Daughters?'

'No daughters. Now all my children are dead.'

'Why did Guru threaten you?'

'He was afraid I might divulge his secret.'

'Did he say so?'

'Yes.'

'Do you think he threatened Senthil also?'

'He may have.'

'Senthil also asked Sita to convey a message to me. He said, "Tell Police Amma I remember everything."'

'He said that?'

'Yes. Sita?'

'He said that just before he said Arumugan could not protect him against Ainthumugan, the Five-faced One. He also said Guru remembered nothing, and he must be told nothing or Ainthumugan would kill him too. I thought he was raving.'

'But he wasn't. Guru's cough syrup was full of insecticide,' Lalli said.

'He punished himself,' Subbu sighed. 'What a fate

is mine! One son an idiot, the other a murderer. Give me my son's body and let me depart. Why can't I get the body now?'

'That's because—'

Lalli broke off to switch on the light. She drew the curtain, revealing the portrait on the wall.

The silence grew tense, anticipant.

Music welled out from somewhere—not too far away, though it was curiously muffled.

Lalli completed the sentence as she turned to face Subbu.

'That's because Brahma's head was cut off. Now it's your turn, Bhagavathar. You have an eager audience. Tell us the story of how Brahma lost his head. Why was he punished? What Purana will you cite? Siva Puranam? Brahma Puranam? Saraswati Puranam? Or, the Puranam of Mani Vadyar? Tell us the story. What was Brahma's crime? Can't remember? Look at this picture, it will remind you. You remember now, don't you? You remember what Brahma did to his daughter?'

Subbu Bhagavathar's terror-stricken eyes seemed mesmerized by the portrait.

'Tell us,' Lalli repeated.

'Yes, tell us!' a new voice asked.

Kamala entered the room.

'Tell us the story of that crime. I have waited twenty years to hear it in your voice. Tell us.'

Her voice was a snarl of contempt and hate.

Subbu Bhagavathar backed away.

Behind him the door had opened silently.

Guru stood in the doorway, violin in hand.

Kamala advanced on Subbu as Guru began playing.

Shyamale meenakshi, sundareshwara sakshi…

With a sob, Kamala turned her face away.

Subbu whirled around. Seeing his son, he bolted towards the balcony where Shukla pinioned him.

'Tell us, Mani Vadyar. Tell us so that your son may hear it. Tell us what Brahma did to his daughter.'

'No, no, don't make me say it,' Subbu fell on his knees, dashing his head on the floor.

'*Tell us what you did to your daughter*.'

'Yes! Yes! I committed Brahma's crime.'

'You raped your daughter.'

'Yes.'

'And when Narayanan told you he had seen Guru, you were terrified of being exposed. What if Guru remembered what he had seen? What if he told Narayanan? What then? You couldn't bear the thought of your brother learning the truth. You picked up the pestle and hit him. You couldn't stop even after you knew he was dead. You kept hitting him till you had vented your hate, your rage, your frustration.'

'If you only knew the burden I have borne all these years!'

'Through the years you made sure Senthil was

drugged most of the time. Every morning you dosed him with that noxious brew. On the morning of the murder you intercepted him when he came home. You knew he would be terrified at the sight of your blood-soaked clothes. You ordered him to exchange clothes with you. If anyone saw you leave in shirt and trousers they wouldn't guess it was you. It would be Narayanan they saw. Senthil could not resist you. Senthil's clothes were certainly a poor fit, but I imagine you managed quite well with an unbuttoned shirt. The trousers are one-size fits all readymades. Senthil did as told, and unquestioningly wore your bloodstained clothes, and you walked away, leaving him there, bewildered.'

'Senthil was mental.'

'You were willing to see him hanged.'

'Senthil was mental.'

'No. Senthil was not mental. He was an innocent and a very intelligent boy,' Ramachandran shouted, bursting into tears. 'He had a divine gift, and you call him mental?'

Dr Q dealt firmly with Ramachandran, and marched him out to the balcony.

Lalli continued. 'You lied about Guru poisoning your wife. You attempted to murder Ramachandran. You probably poisoned Senthil's already poisonous kashayam—I have no proof of that. But you committed all these crimes to conceal the crime you could not admit to. Admit it now. Did you rape your daughter?'

'I did not harm her.'

'Did you rape your daughter?'

'I did not mean to harm her.'

'What happened on the night of 1st October 1995?'

'I will tell you,' Guru's voice said. 'I remember everything now, since Senthil died. I think Senthil remembered it too. We were seven, Senthil and I. Akka—our sister Kamakshi, was thirteen. Two nights ago I'd woken up to hear her crying. I asked her what the matter was, but she wouldn't say. Senthil told me she was being crushed by our father. That's the word he used. That's what we thought. We thought he was crushing our Akka. On that night—if it was 1st October, I don't remember the date, but I do remember what happened. Senthil woke me up. We saw our father crushing Akka, and Akka struggling beneath his weight. Then somehow she got free. Senthil sat up, and she saw we were both awake. I remember her eyes blazing with fear. She dashed out of the room, onto the balcony. Father went after her. To escape him, she climbed the railing and jumped. Senthil and I rushed to the railing and watched her fall. Senthil screamed for our mother. Father told us he would kill us if we said a word to her. We didn't, not then. Two days later, Senthil told her everything. When we woke up, our mother was gone. Father told us she had died of fever, but we didn't believe him. We decided to run away to find our mother, but

Senthil was so small and weak, I told him I would go and bring her back. So I ran away.'

Lalli turned away, making a sign to Shukla and Savio. Shaktivel had two constables waiting, and the door closed on Subbu Bhagavathar.

I was trembling, not at what I had just witnessed, but at the memory of Senthil's last hour.

His every word and gesture stood explained now.

The scene replayed itself:

Senthil asks Ramachandran to sing, invoking his beloved Murugan.

Ramachandran sings, and Senthil sees his vision of six-faced Murugan and cries out, 'Arumuga!'

Ramachandran is singing a plaintive melody, one of yearning for the Lord. Senthil mimes the song, tears spilling unchecked, his face contorted with pain.

When Ramachandran falls silent, Senthil says, 'Tell Police Amma I remember everything.'

He had remembered that October night in all its ghastly detail.

When I had asked him to explain, he had retreated behind his mantra of sanity and survival: *Anbe Sivam*.

I wept now as I thought how earnestly he had lived out that gentle philosophy through his brief caged life. It had strengthened him enough to break past the numbing kashayam, and the burden of memory. His life had been neither as simple nor tranquil as it had appeared to his friends at the temple. It had gained in intensity with every declamation of poetry and song.

I returned to that moment when he had repeated his mantra.

'Anbe Sivam.'

I am mistaken. This is no retreat. The mantra is now a command. The words are a vel, piercing his illusions, prompting him to cry out the truth he has just recalled.

The truth is too cruel, too horrible to be borne, and he cries out in reproach to his beloved Murugan: 'Arumuga, could you not protect me from the five-faced one?'

It is his own devastated life he sees, the long desolation brought about by his father, now codified as Brahma, the five-faced one.

Even while facing the truth, Senthil cannot deny his father's power. A fallen god, but a god still. The truth can only be viewed through Senthil's usual plane of reality. Subbu's crime is still mythic: metaphor, not fact.

Senthil is attempting to free himself, though. Desperately, he wants to convince me of this new reality. He reminds me repeatedly to tell Lalli: 'It was Ainthumugan, the five-faced one.'

From that moment on, Senthil becomes urgently practical. His first concern is Guru. 'Don't tell him, or the five-faced one will kill him too!'

But the truth is unstoppable now, a rock rolling downhill. All of it must be known. Senthil must discover more. He needs the vel to pierce his illusions again, he needs his beloved Arumugan. He urges Ramachandran, 'Call him again!'

And Ramachandran does.

By now, Ramachandran is aware of Senthil's truth, he has grasped the terrible meaning of the five-faced one.

He too is being compelled, like Senthil, towards discovery. The pressure of it tells in his flushed and sweating face, in the halting tremolo of the song—and then he is swept by the sound, into the song itself.

Senthil, clutching Ramachandran's hand, is transported to the moment of arrival, as Arumugan hovers, visible at last.

Va, velava, vadivelava, mayil meedu nee va, Kumara, va!

At this point, I notice Senthil's eyes change. The look of exaltation leaves his face. It becomes alert, intent. His eyes focus on—what?

The god who has arrived is a young man, resplendent and glorious. His peacock casts its shadow on the stone flags where he has alighted. The last syllable of the *Kandan kavacham* trembles on Senthil's lips.

Senthil's eyes are now watching not myth, but memory.

He is in the courtyard of the temple at Ambarnath, watching the Mayil Azhagan.

Suddenly a cry rings out.

The last syllable of the kavacham is lost to Senthil.

Past the Mayil Azhagan's glittering presence, Senthil sees the truth.

He catches a glimpse of the woman convulsing across the courtyard, and recognizes her.

This is the memory Senthil sees. He cries out in recognition, in jubilation, 'Amma!'

And dies.

What had happened to Senthil after that brief recognition at Ambarnath? I had seen him at that moment. He was the slight young man I had noticed through the Mayil Azhagan's shining panoply. And then I had not seen him again.

Had that moment quickly retreated again into obscurity? For certain, Senthil had retained no memory of that joy till it returned as his last and enduring truth.

During my own retreat into Senthil's last hour, everyone else in the room too had retreated into a private recall. Our faces are shut to visitors, as Kamala's has been for twenty years.

Vinyasam

Kamala began to speak. 'It all happened more or less as Guru said. I have told Lalli what happened after that, but I will repeat it now, adding what I have now realized.'

She spoke in English, hesitating before each phrase as though the long habit of silence had robbed her tongue of will.

'After Senthil told me this… I said nothing to my husband.'

Tears streamed down her tired face.

'Guru is here, but Senthil! Senthil! I am the true criminal, not that man you have arrested. Why did I leave? I can't understand it. I just knew I had to get away. I gathered all the money in the house, stuffed some clothes into a bag and stole out of the house. How will you ever forgive me, Guru!'

She broke down in agony. Guru placed a hesitant hand on her arm. The gesture told us this was the first time he had touched his mother since their reunion.

Kamala wiped her tears and continued. 'I wanted to get as far away from my misery as I could. I took a taxi to Dadar station. I bought a ticket to Kanyakumari—why? It was either that or Kashmir. The journey went like a flash. I left the station, looked around, knowing there would be a choultry where I could get a bath before going to the temple.

I had a purpose. I was going to see her. She would be there, waiting!'

She stopped abruptly, her clenched face unfolding in gradual realization.

'It was evening. I bought jasmine with the pink roses she loved, braided with tulsi, for her long beautiful hair. She had two thick plaits that swung over her shoulders when she ran, she wanted—oh so much—pink satin ribbons, and I never got them for her.

'I went into the temple, and there she was, returned to me, standing in the golden haze of lamps, jagatjyoti, my child, my daughter, my own Kamakshi! How sweet her smile was, so full of mischief and delight! She had a new dress, pink, her favourite pink. I had pink roses. I could go out and buy the ribbons here, I should have bought them, I told her, but she just laughed, saying it didn't matter, nothing mattered, she was here, happy and free and nobody could hurt her again—

'And then I saw him, the coarse rascal I had married. He turned to the crowd around me, undressing one woman after another with his eyes. Hadn't I seen him looking at his students like this? Stop it, I told him so many times, stop it, can't you see the girls notice? Can't you see how many students have dropped out? But he laughed and said he was doing no harm, it was only innocent fun. Innocent!'

Kamala stopped and transfixed Lalli with a long intent look. Lalli held her gaze, unflinching.

'You were there, Lalli! You saw him. I saw your rage as his eyes swept you. You saw me. Our eyes met, but I didn't remember you then, and neither did you recognize me.

'He looked at me, sending a spasm of disgust through me. I was married to him, to this ignorant brute with a voice like a hog's, daring to call his grunting music! For fifteen years he had gagged me. I used to sit next to him on the dais and scrape the fiddle, trying to drown his graceless singing. Ugh—I don't know what disgusted me most, his lechery or his ignorance. And to set himself up as a teacher—it was too much. And he was the father of my children. He was her father. *Her father.*'

Kamala spoke through clenched teeth, her musical voice sinking to a raspy growl. 'Her *father*. He stood there, raping us, his veshti too flimsy to hide his shame—and then. And then, he turned his filthy gaze on *her*.'

Kamala's voice rose, incantatory, oracular. 'He turned on her. On my daughter, on his daughter, on our daughter, laughing at us in her innocence, standing tiptoe to twirl her new pink skirt. He turned his lecherous eyes on her. I knew then what I must do.

'I left the temple, leaving her there, leaving my Kamakshi, knowing she would be safe from him as long as there was a crowd around. I ran out and bought a knife. When I left the shop, we saw each other again, Lalli. I was to remember that later.

'I went back into the temple. He was no longer in there, he was on his way out. I caught sight of him. He would hurry away now, stealing in the dark to her bed as he had been doing—oh God, for how long!

'I hid in the corridor near the elephants, knowing he would have to walk that way soon, there was no other exit. One man walked past, two, three in a group. Not him.

'And then he came. I waited till he was level with me, then I sprang at him with the knife, using all my strength I rammed it between his ribs. It knocked the wind out of him, and he fell at the elephant's feet. The animal, disturbed, trumpeted as I fled. I walked away quickly, joining the crowd. I felt no remorse, only relief. My daughter was safe now. I hurried to the station and bought a ticket home. The train left in half an hour. I could be home with the boys in two days.

'And then, Lalli, I saw you. I saw you with two policemen in the station, waiting for the train. And I remembered where I had seen you before. Not at the temple, but in my home long ago, on Deepavali day before the boys were born. You've not forgotten, either.

'I saw you—and the truth hit me. The man I had

killed was not my husband. My husband was still at home, still in the house that rang with my daughter's screams. I had done nothing for Kamakshi. I had killed an innocent man. Perhaps I had imagined his lechery, perhaps it was real, but what was that to me?

'I got on the train because I had to leave the place. I shut my eyes, willing myself to be silent, to think. A commotion roused me. A child in the upper berth had high fever, and now he had developed fits. The parents were desperate—and very ignorant. The boy was the same age as my sons. I took care of him. The parents were very grateful, but I kept up my silence, accepting their kindness, but showing by signs that I could not speak. It seemed the safest thing to do, the only way I could avoid questions. The train reached Bombay. I kept sitting in the compartment. The child's parents approached me with concern. I signed that I had nowhere to go. They took me home with them.

'They were poor village people, rag pickers in a slum in Dharavi. I stayed with them. It was a new life, a silent life, a violent life in that slum, but I had found kindness, even love. I made friends gradually. I have some skill in making snacks. I started a small murukku business with my friend Mayamma. She put in money, I did the job. Five years later, we moved to Kanchpada.

'Life went on. Then this year, as usual I went with

my friends for Panguni Uthiram, walking with the Kavadi bearers at the temple at Ambarnath. There I heard a voice singing *Kandar kavacham* so sweetly, I turned to look, and I saw this boy—half hidden behind the Mayil Azhagan. My sons would be as old as this boy—grief overwhelmed me. They say the spirit entered me, but I have no belief in such things!

'Still, when I recovered, I decided I would go and look for my sons. And one afternoon, I did. But the old place was long gone, nobody knew them there. Nobody knew *me*! In my new life, I've learned to dress differently, wearing my sari this Tamil way.

'And then you came, Lalli, and sang the song I used to sing to my Kamakshi, just the way I used to sing it. How she used to giggle when I teased her with it. Aah—' A long drawn out cry of pain escaped her.

'I remembered then, Lalli, the first time we met. I knew then you had understood my life in an instant. My bitterness, my misery, my helplessness in that marriage to this brute. There, my story is done. Do whatever needs to be done. If I can make any reparation to the family of the man I killed, tell me how, and I will do it.'

'Let Guru take you home,' Lalli said. 'Get to know your son. In a few days, we will tell you what needs to be done.'

'But don't I have to go to jail?'

'No,' Shukla said.

'Not yet,' Lalli amended.

'I'll be back,' Guru said as they left. 'If you still want to hear that capriccio.'

'We do,' Ramachandran said.

Kamala stopped at the door. She took something from her bag and walked back, to place it on the table.

'I think this belongs to you,' she told Lalli.

It was a delicate white and gold conch.

When Guru and Kamala had left, Lalli stood for a moment in the middle of the room, looking at us helplessly. The moment was so brief that apart from Dr Q, nobody noticed it. Each of us was too absorbed in the sudden deceleration of shocking events, a kind of free fall that threatened to be endless.

Dr Q got up just as Lalli seemed to have come to some decision.

She said, 'Now you know the truth. It's not an excuse, but I want to tell you why I committed murder. The reason goes back seven years from that evening in Kumari, to the Deepavali morning in Kamala's house. When I watched her with Kamakshi, it was evident the child was the closest thing to her soul. The sight reminded me of my own loss, for I had known such intense love too. But I had lost it, and for years I had kept up a semblance of survival by denying my pain. When I saw Kamala again at

Kanyakumari, I was reminded again of my own loss. I still couldn't bear to confront it. And so I forgot the moment. I forgot what I had just witnessed. I committed murder.'

'You didn't, Lalli,' Savio said in a low voice.

'I did. It was my crime. I was there. I saw it all. I even knew before the fact. I saw her buy the knife. I knew her intent. I heard about the murder a few days later. I was silent. I did nothing.'

'But do you know why?' Savio asked.

'I've just told you why. You have some other explanation?'

'Yes. So does Kamala. You had read Kamala's story without knowing it. Your previous encounter had told you everything about her life, everything about Mani Vadyar. Of Kamakshi's rape you could not have known, but you felt the mother's anguish as the pujari turned to the goddess. You knew she saw not the goddess, but her own daughter. And you understood.'

'Does that make it less of a crime?'

'Yes,' said Dr Q.

'Now you are committing crime by opening the file,' Shukla said. 'Now if you put this mother in jail, it is a crime.'

'Ramachandran?'

'We are not a jury of your peers, Lalli,' Ramachandran said gently. 'But since you ask me—'

He began to sing the haunting song that had restored Lalli's memory.

Kaumari, gowri, velavali—

But now his voice had a different loft, as the notes rose, pneum by pneum, in breaths of beauty:

Gaana lole, susheele baale!

Now the song brought not memory, but command. The notes rose imperiously, as if this Baala, this child, any child, were charging us, rough blundering adults all, to keep her inviolate and divine.

A Note on the Musical Terms

The system of music codified in the sixteenth century in south India is called 'Carnatic' today.

It is based on musical systems developed in India—both the northern stream and that of the ancient Sangam culture of Tamilakam.

It is enriched further by musical systems from all over the world—a trend that is energetically pursued today. It is, above all, music for a lifetime. It starts out very young and explores vicissitudes growing in strength with maturity, subtly becoming both thought, idiom and expression.

Young musicians today recognize its potential as a global language to be developed, not merely a tradition to be cherished. Their brilliant innovations and courageous explorations make Carnatic music the idiom of hope in a world increasingly polarized by hate and violence.

This novel uses a few words and phrases peculiar to Carnatic music. I hope this skeletal explanation will prompt readers to experience the music for themselves—the Internet awaits!

Swaram: Musical note.

Raagam: A melodic progression of notes.

Raagams mentioned in this novel:

Mohanam
Dwijawanti
Shanmukhapriya
Kapi
Khamas
Kharaharapriya
Shivaranjani
Saurashtram

Raagam Taanam Pallavi: A performance that explores the melodic structure of a *raagam*, relying heavily on improvisations called Manodharma. It demands concentration, imagination and expertise, and is the benchmark of competence in Carnatic music.

Raagam: Here the word denotes *raga-alapanai*: exploring and developing the notes, defining the architecture of the *raagam*, but also subtly challenging it.

Taanam: Exploration of the sounds within a *raagam* using the repetition of the syllables *Ananta-Anandam-Ta* (Give me bliss, Infinite One).

Pallavi: Lyrical exposition. The word is a composite of the first syllables of its component parts: (*Padam*: phrase; *Layam*: tempo; *Vinyasam*: variations).

In a *Raagam Taanam Pallavi*, the *pallavi* is usually a single line of lyric which is explored in musical variations.

Alapanai: Introductory exploration of a *raagam*.

Niraval: Melodic variations on a single (usually felicitous) phrase or line of lyric.

Kelvi gnanam: Musical smarts without formal training.

Kriti: (Lit: Composition.) Format of Carnatic song. A *kriti* embodies both lyric and tune. While it has a definite structure, each part can be exploited for melodic exploration. A *kriti's* lyric and music (usually both) are attributed to the composer whose signature, or *'mudra'* appears in the lyric. Muthuswami Dikshitar's *Mudra* is *Guruguha*.

Several *kritis* have been mentioned in this novel. They are all popular compositions, and can be heard on the Internet.

Viraha Geet: Music of separation and yearning.

Thillana: Rhythmic composition usually performed at the end of a concert.

Tamil words used in the text:

Pattu pavadai: Traditional festive dress for little girls: a floor-length silk skirt.

Rasikan: Connoisseur.

Murukku: (Lit: Twist) Generic for a variety of crisp savouries.

Kai murukku: Murukku plaited in circles.

Mayil kazhuthu: (Lit: peacock neck) blue green shot silk.

Panneer: *Guettrada speciosa,* a medicinal tree, endemic to the Western Ghats.

Elai adai: Dumpling steamed in banana leaf.

ALSO IN THIS SERIES BY KALPANA SWAMINATHAN

MURDER IN SEVEN ACTS

LALLI MYSTERIES

Kalpana Swaminathan

Lalli, retired policewoman, intrepid detective, collects curiosities... that inevitably lead to murder.

The curiosity of murder unfolds in seven acts.

Since Kalpana Swaminathan's first whodunit was published over ten years ago, Lalli—sixty and silver-haired and tough as nails—has been one of the most memorable detectives in Indian fiction. Lalli returns in this brilliant page-turner, a collection of seven stories, to solve some of the strangest, most complex cases of her career.

The opening act, in which a face keeps reappearing until a crime committed long ago is revealed, is followed by a murder that could be hypothetical—or a reality (Lalli turns to Schrodinger's Cat to find out). In the third act in this unfolding drama, Lalli and Sita are invited to a book-burning which turns out to be murder most foul. And Lalli turns her skills to the world of high fashion when Sita sits next to a serial killer on a bus—but was he killer or victim?

The aptly named Suicide Point in Bombay's suburbs, leads Lalli to a suicide that turns out to be something far more sinister. And an innocuous desk ornament is the clue to a crime most artistically executed. Finally, for connoisseurs of fiction, the curtains come down with a threnody for lost love.

Page Extent: 224 pp | Price: ₹399